The Five D's

---

how to grow in your relationship with Jesus

DECISION

DELIVERED

DUNKED

DISCIPLED

DEPLOYED

robert herber

THE FIVE D'S

Copyright © 2020 Robert Herber

All rights reserved. No portion of this book may be reproduced, stored in a retrieval system, or transmitted in any form or by any means—electronic, mechanical, photocopy, recording, scanning, or other—except for brief quotations in critical reviews or articles, or as specifically allowed by the U. S. Copyright Act of 1976, as amended, without the prior written permission of the publisher.

Published by Clear Day Publishing, a division of Clear Day Media Group LLC, Waco, TX, cleardaypublishing.com.

Published in association with Lux Creative {theluxcreative.com}

Unless otherwise noted, Scripture quotations are taken from the New American Standard Bible®, Copyright © 1960, 1962, 1963, 1968, 1971, 1972, 1973, 1975, 1977, 1995 by The Lockman Foundation. Used by permission. (www.Lockman.org)

Quotations designated NIV are from The Holy Bible, New International Version®, NIV® Copyright © 1973, 1978, 1984, 2011 by Biblica, Inc.® Used by permission. All rights reserved worldwide.

Quotations designated NKJV are taken from the New King James Version®. Copyright © 1982 by Thomas Nelson, Inc. Used by permission. All rights reserved.

Quotations designated ESV are taken from The Holy Bible, English Standard Version® (ESV®) Copyright © 2001 by Crossway, a publishing ministry of Good News Publishers. All rights reserved. ESV Text Edition: 2011

ISBN: 978-1-7326252-7-3
Library of Congress Control Number: 2020918981

Cover Design: Carolynn Seibert
Interior Design: Lux Creative {theluxcreative.com}

Printed in the United States of America.

CONTENTS

CHAPTER ONE: The First "D" — *Decision* 3

CHAPTER TWO: Introducing the 5 Ds 11

CHAPTER THREE: The Second "D"— *Dunked* (Baptism) 19

CHAPTER FOUR: The Third "D"— *Delivered* 29

CHAPTER FIVE: The Fourth "D" — *Discipled* 43

CHAPTER SIX: The Fifth "D" — *Deployed* 59

PARTING THOUGHTS 71

SMALL GROUP / MENTOR DISCUSSION QUESTIONS 73

Chapter One

THE FIRST "D"
Decision

One decision can change your whole life.

Things weren't going as planned. We were supposed to take the commuter train to downtown Chicago, then ride the elevator to the observation floor of the Sears building, the city's tallest structure. There, gazing upon Chicago's famous skyline, I would take the leap of faith that had consumed me for weeks.

But now, an uncharacteristic fog had descended on the city, with reports claiming zero visibility. I had to make a game time decision. I was nervous to the point of being nauseated. Could I really do this? If I did, everything would change. This one decision would dramatically alter every part of my life.

I quickly changed plans and we ventured into a park on the shoreline of Lake Michigan. It was completely unfamiliar, it was cold and windy, and I felt like my heart would beat out of my chest. In that moment, I made my decision. With more courage than I'd ever needed before, I got down on my knee, pulled out a ring, and did the deed that's been done millions of times before in millions of ways throughout history. I invited my beautiful girlfriend, Stefanie Herman, to share the rest of her life with me.

She said yes, and nothing has ever been the same. I went from being single to having a constant companion. I went from having my own bedroom to sharing one. I went from having my own bank account to a joint one. I went from deciding my own schedule to shaping each day with another person. No longer my own, my life now belonged to another person. In that moment we launched into an amazing adventure that has grown and developed month after month, year after year.

There is only one decision in my life that has been more important or has had greater consequences than that one: the decision to say yes to Jesus when he called me to follow him. Nothing has ever been the same.

IT'S ALL ABOUT JESUS

Jesus is the most amazing person who ever walked this earth. Many people don't realize the entire Bible teaches about Jesus. Jesus has been written about more than any other historical figure. As you read this, over two and a half billion people from across the earth have made the same decision I made to follow him—that's over a third of the world's population. Why?

Jesus walked the earth over 2000 years ago and changed the course of history, but He was more than a historical figure, a great leader, a revolutionary, or the founder of a movement. Jesus is the God who created you and the One who gave his life so that you could have a personal relationship with Him. When Jesus came to earth as a man, He taught with incredible wisdom, healed the sick, raised the dead, set people free from demonic oppression and showed compassion to the poor. People loved being around Him and dropped everything—their businesses, their families, their friends and homes — to follow Him.

There has never been anyone like Jesus. You may be reading this book because you have decided to follow Him or you are thinking about it. This is the best decision you could ever make. Jesus will meet you in the tiny minutia of your life and make you a part of His grand purpose for the world. Jesus will not only save you, but will also heal you, give your life meaning, satisfy your deepest longings and help you make sense of your daily struggles.

Think about it. The Bible says that one day every knee will bow before Jesus, but today He holds out His hand to you personally, promising you a full life you can't find anywhere else (John 10:10). When you say yes to Jesus, He takes you on a journey of transformation that begins with a new spirituality, a new identity, a new purity and a new destiny. Let's unpack those.

A NEW SPIRITUALITY

In a conversation Jesus had with His disciples shortly before He was crucified, He told them this:

I will ask the Father, and he will give you another advocate to help you and be with you forever—the Spirit of truth. The world cannot accept him, because it neither sees him nor knows him. But you know him, for he lives with you and will be in you. (John 15:16-18)

When we decide to follow Jesus, He promises to put His Spirit inside of us, breathing life into our souls. Here's why this is so important. According to the Bible, when we come into the world, the spirit inside of us is not only dead, but Satan is always working to get us to follow him and disobey God by "gratifying the cravings of our flesh and following its desires and thoughts" (Ephesians 2:1-3).

This is a pretty ugly picture, and not what God wants for us. But this passage goes on to say: "But because of his great love for us, God, who is rich in mercy, made us alive with Christ even when we were dead in transgressions—it is by grace you have been saved" (Ephesians 2:4-5). Jesus called this process being "born again" because it brings such a radical change in us (See John 3:3-8). Because of God's mercy and love, He sends His Spirit to live in us and change us from the inside out. Not only will we never be alone again, but Satan also loses his power over our hearts. This is our new spirituality.

A NEW IDENTITY

When Jesus promised His disciples that He would send His Spirit,

He added, "I will not leave you as orphans; I will come to you" (John 14:19). Let me just tell you—when you follow Jesus, His Spirit comes in and gives you a new identity as His child. One of Jesus' disciples explained it this way: "See what great love the Father has lavished on us, that we should be called children of God! And that is what we are!" (1 John 3:1). God, who created the heavens and the earth, is now your Dad and He loves you more than you can imagine!

Perhaps you've never really known your earthly father, or your relationship has been painful. God is different from every other father because He is perfect in all His ways. The Scriptures tell us that our heavenly Father is always "compassionate and gracious, slow to anger, abounding in love" (Psalm 103:8). He actually thinks about you continually and even rejoices over you with singing (Psalm 139, Zephaniah 3:17).

I am an imperfect dad, but I love my kids so much that at times I can hardly contain it. Every night I am home, I tuck them in and kiss them on the forehead, telling them I love them — even my teenagers (I don't care if it embarrasses them)! I wake them each morning with a gentle touch and say, "Good morning man of God!" to my sons and "Good morning beautiful!" to my daughter. If I treat my children like this, as an imperfect dad, how much more does your Father in heaven want to express his affection to you! You can rest assured: you are no orphan. You are never alone. You now are a child of God. That is who you are.

A NEW PURITY

One of my favorite stories of Jesus' life is when some religious leaders brought a woman that they'd caught in sexual immorality to Him. They knew Jesus had a reputation for being compassionate, and since their law required stoning for her sins, they were clearly trying to set him up. As the story goes, Jesus paused and wrote in the dirt with His finger, then looked up and told them: "Let any one of you who is without sin be the first to throw a stone at her (John 8:7). What could they say to that? One by one they slipped away until only Jesus and the woman were left. He looked at her and asked: "Woman, where are they? Has no one condemned you?" (v. 10). When she told him no, Jesus responded, "Then neither do I condemn you. Go now and leave your life of sin" (v. 11).

Did you know that Jesus did not come to condemn you for your sins either, but to save you from them? (John 3:17). The Scriptures tell us clearly that we've all sinned in so many ways — lying, cheating, stealing, lusting, coveting — even adultery or murder: "For all have sinned and fall short of the glory of God" (Romans 3:23). Because of that, we deserve to die (Romans 6:23). But Jesus gave his life to pay for your sins and mine, so that just like the woman caught in adultery, we can "go and sin no more" (John 8:11).

Because of Jesus' death, God sees you as beautifully pure. He forgives you of everything you've done in the past and then promises that "If we confess our sins, he is faithful and just and will forgive us our sins and purify us from all unrighteousness" (1 John 1:9). It is as if you stand before a judge, knowing you are in the wrong, but hearing him proclaim over your life: "Not guilty!" You have a new purity.

A NEW DESTINY

There's a lot of talk today about how important it is to plan our futures, to know where we are going and to plan out how we will get there. But how many people go through life not knowing their eternal destiny? This is tragic. Jesus taught very clearly that every person will end up in one of two places — heaven or hell, describing hell as a place where "the fire is never quenched and there is weeping or gnashing of teeth" (See Matthew 8:12, 13:42, 50; Matthew 22:13, 24:51, 25:30 and Luke 13:28). Hell is the place reserved for those who reject God's gift of eternal life through Jesus Christ.

But Jesus told His disciples: "Because I live, you also will live" (John 15:19). When you decide to follow Jesus, you gain a new destiny — heaven! We can't even begin to imagine the wonder of eternal life in heaven. Most importantly, it is where Jesus lives and reigns and where we will see him face to face, surrounded by scores of angels. Because all who put their trust in Him find their home in heaven, we will see friends and relatives who have followed Jesus there — it will be a grand reunion!

In a beautiful description of heaven, Scripture tells us it is a place where there are no more tears, no more sickness or disease, no more killing or death! In heaven we will experience unending peace, fullness of joy, perfect health, and the perfection of nature. Heaven is one of the greatest gifts we who follow Jesus look forward to!

But we don't have to wait until we die to experience this incredible destiny. Jesus said: "Now this is eternal life: that they know you, the only true God, and Jesus Christ, whom you have sent" (John 17:3). The minute Jesus comes into your life, you have the privilege of getting to know him — a journey that He called the abundant life, and it includes all the benefits we will experience fully in eternity. Knowing Jesus is your destiny, one that begins the minute you decide to give your life to Him, and it will get better and better until the day you enter the gates of heaven and bow before Him.

NAILING IT DOWN

I hope you can see that there is nothing better than giving your life to Jesus. When you decide to follow Him, you have everything to gain and nothing to lose. Maybe as you've read this chapter, you're not sure whether you've made the decision to say yes and receive Jesus into your life as Lord and Savior. If not, why not settle it once and for all right now? If you want to begin a journey of knowing Jesus and receiving all that He has for you, stop now and pray the following prayer:

Dear Jesus, I need you. Thank you for dying on the cross for me. I repent of my sins. Please forgive me. Thank you rising from the dead. I am deciding to follow you now. Please be my Lord and my Savior. I receive your gift of the Holy Spirit. Please fill me. Amen.

If you prayed that prayer and truly meant it, you have made the greatest decision you will ever make! Congratulations and welcome to your new life!

This is the beginning of your destiny! Get ready for an amazing ride!

SHARING THE JOURNEY

The best way to experience all God has for you is to share it with a friend or mentor or as a part of a life group. Please see the discussion guide on page 73 for you to use with fellow travelers.

Chapter Two

INTRODUCING THE 5 *D*s

Let me begin by saying that following Jesus is not like anything you've ever experienced. In fact, a lot of people have the wrong idea about it. Let me give you an example. Often on a Friday night, we will surprise our kids by taking them to see a good family movie. It's nice to just sit back, relax, escape the pressures of the week and enjoy the show. There is something about the cushioned stadium seats, massive screen, and surround sound that can't be beat. For a lot of people, following Jesus looks kind of like that. When you head to church or even watch it online — you sit back, enjoy the show and are done until the next time.

Although you get to see God do many amazing things, just sitting back and enjoying the show is not what church or following Jesus is all about. His plan is a lot more like joining a gym than going to the movies. Think about it. You go to a theatre to be entertained, but you go to a gym to be trained. You go to a theatre to escape, but you go to a gym to get in shape.

Do you get this? Following Jesus is not just enjoying the show — it's being in the middle of the action. It means learning what Jesus taught and doing what He said. It means being transformed from the inside out so that you don't fall apart when things get tough. It's means building your life on the only thing that will last. Jesus described it this way:

Therefore everyone who hears these words of mine and puts them into practice is like a wise man who built his house on the rock. The rain came down, the streams rose, and the winds blew and beat against that house; yet it did not fall, because it had its foundation on the rock. But everyone who hears these words of mine and does not put them into practice is like a foolish man who built his house on sand. The rain came down, the streams rose, and the winds blew and beat against that house, and it fell with a great crash Matthew 7:24-27

Jesus is the Rock you can build your life on, but it doesn't happen automatically — you have a part to play. That's what this book is all about. We believe Jesus has a clear action plan for you to follow, a growth path we call the "5 D's." These five steps from Scripture will be your training program:

- **Decision**
- **Dunked**
- **Delivered**
- **Discipled**
- **Deployed**

For the rest of this chapter we are going to look at someone whose world got turned upside down when he met Jesus. As I walk through the 5 Ds in his life, ask yourself where you are with each one so you can see what your next step is in following Jesus. If you have completed all five, you'll see how to bring others with you on this amazing journey with Jesus.

AN UNLIKELY ROLE MODEL

In the 1970s and 80s at the height of rock and roll music, there was a phrase that people used when they had been utterly impacted by something: "That rocked me!" You can't meet Jesus without getting rocked. That's why we've coined this slogan at All Peoples Church: "Get rocked, get real, and give it away." That's what happened to a man named Saul (later called Paul) who got so rocked by Jesus that He left everything behind, started a slew of churches and ended up writing much of the New Testament.

First, the backstory. After Jesus died and rose again, He hung out with His disciples, teaching them about what was to come. He promised that although He was going back to heaven, He would send the Holy Spirit to baptize them with the power they would need. When that happened on Pentecost, the church was born. 3000 people got saved in one day, and things just exploded from there. Then this angry dude with a lot of power showed up:

Meanwhile, Saul was still breathing out murderous threats against the Lord's disciples. He went to the high priest and asked him for letters to the synagogues in Damascus, so that if he found any there who belonged to the Way, whether men or women, he might take them as prisoners to Jerusalem." (Acts 9:1-2)

Saul, a Jewish leader, hated Jesus' followers, so he was having some people thrown in prison and others killed. As a side note, hopefully you know this by now, but Jesus isn't looking for "good," "nice" or "perfect" people. He reaches out to the most sinful and unlikely looking folks and invites them to follow Him. Here's how He got Saul's attention:

As he neared Damascus on his journey, suddenly a light from heaven flashed around him. He fell to the ground and heard a voice say to him, "Saul, Saul, why do you persecute me?"

"Who are you, Lord?" Saul asked.

"I am Jesus, whom you are persecuting," he replied. "Now get up and go into the city, and you will be told what you must do." (Acts 9:3-6)

Imagine this scene. Everyone who is with Saul hears God's voice, so they're all looking around, probably freaked out because they can't see where the sound came from. Saul stumbles to his feet, only to discover that he can't see a thing. His companions take his hand and lead him to the nearest town. The Scriptures tell us that for the next three days Saul did not eat or drink a thing (verses 7-9). Jesus had rocked his world.

DECISION

An encounter with Jesus always calls for a response. What was Saul's? He addresses Jesus as Lord and then does exactly what He tells him to do. It is clear this guy wants what Jesus has for him. He has made a decision to follow Him.

Meanwhile, the drama is playing out not far away with a Jesus follower named Ananias, whom God appears to in a vision, telling him to go to the specific house where Saul is staying. God assures Ananias that Saul will be ready because he's had a vision of Ananias praying over him and restoring his sight.

Of course, Ananias is terrified—wouldn't you be? Every Christian far and wide knew about this vicious murderer named Saul. But God astonishes Ananias with an amazing prophecy about how Saul is His chosen instrument to proclaim his name outside of the Jewish community. So, Ananias goes and prays over Saul, saying: "Brother Saul, the Lord — Jesus, who appeared to you on the road as you were coming here — has sent me so that you may see again and be filled with the Holy Spirit" (Acts 9:17).

DUNKED

The story goes on to say: "Immediately, something like scales fell from Saul's eyes, and he could see again. He got up and was baptized, and after taking some food, he regained his strength" (Acts 9:18-19). The very first thing Saul does after being healed is get baptized, a word that literally means "submerged" or as we say, "dunked"! (Okay, it's a little cheesy, but we needed a "D" and this works!) Baptism is a great picture of what God has done in giving us new life: "Therefore, if anyone is in Christ, the new creation has come: The old has gone, the new is here!" (2 Corinthians 5:17).

In a sermon to a bunch of new followers of Jesus in the Bible, Peter tells them that their next step is to repent and be baptized (Acts 2:38). We will discuss it more in detail in the next chapter, but if you have made the decision to invite Jesus Christ to be your Lord and Savior, then your next step is to be baptized.

Many people have given their lives to Christ but have never been baptized. If this is you, now is the time! Sometimes people who were baptized as babies wonder if that counts. As meaningful as that event may have been to your parents, they were dedicating you — it wasn't your decision. True baptism takes place after you have made the decision to trust in Christ and have experienced the new birth by His Spirit.

But baptism by water isn't the only way God wants to immerse us. Later we will see how Jesus promises to baptize us in the Holy Spirit and to baptize us with fire, some pretty incredible experiences.

DELIVERED

When Ananias laid his hands on Saul and prayed, the Bible says that "scales fell from Saul's eyes, and he could see again" (Acts 9:18)." We know that Saul received his physical sight, but this is also a picture of what happens when God removes the scales from our spiritual eyes, and we can see the things that have been keeping us from experiencing the abundant life Jesus promised and be set free from them. That's our third "D" – *delivered.*

So many people are dealing with various types of bondage, suffering from despair, hopelessness and suicidal thoughts. Scores of people have visible addictions such as drugs, alcohol, pornography, and gambling, while other people are addicted to more acceptable vices like food, media, gaming, and shopping. Anger, bitterness, unforgiveness and anxiety control people's lives and relationships. This is not how it is supposed to be.

Jesus explained his mission on this earth in this way: The Spirit of the Lord is on me, because he has anointed me to proclaim good news to the poor. He has sent me to proclaim freedom for the prisoners and recovery of sight for the blind, to set the oppressed free" Luke 4:18. How amazing is that? Jesus came to heal you in all the ways Satan has tried to hold you down. The scripture says he "went about doing good and healing all who were oppressed by the devil, for God was with him" (Acts 10:38). Jesus is for you. He wants to bless you, deliver you from oppression and set you free, and that is really good news.

DISCIPLED

Back to our story, which tells us that "Saul spent several days with the disciples in Damascus." (Acts 9:19) This simple statement says a lot about what we need once we've been rocked by Jesus. Saul was dunked, then delivered and now he is being discipled, which is our fourth step in God's growth path.

One of the reasons that many churches are more like a movie theater than a gym today is that they have no training. In a gym, when you want to up your game, you hire a personal trainer, someone who can help you learn how to practice the moves and use the right equipment to get in top shape. In the church, we call that being *discipled*. Discipleship is intentional training.

There are two ways discipleship takes place, and Jesus demonstrated both. First, He spent a lot of time with a small group of people who traveled around with Him. You also need to have a community of people with whom to practice your faith. In a small group community, you learn how to study the Word, pray, develop committed Christian friendships, use your spiritual gifts, and meet each other's needs. This is what the very first home groups in the early church looked like:

> *They devoted themselves to the apostles' teaching and to fellowship, to the breaking of bread and to prayer. Everyone was filled with awe at the many wonders and signs performed by the apostles. All the believers were together and had everything in common. (Acts 2:42-43)*

As great as a large church service can be, it can never provide the atmosphere for training that a small group offers. So, the first way to get discipled is to join a small group.

The second way to receive intentional training is through a mentoring relationship with a more mature believer. Jesus took three of the disciples away many times so He could give them more personal training. Even Saul, who wrote about many powerful encounters with Jesus in the New Testament, needed a mentor. God gave him a man named Barnabas to guide and encourage him in his faith. Doesn't it make sense that if the great Apostle Paul needed a mentor, then we do too?

A mentor is someone you can learn from, someone who will not only share truth with you, but show you how to put it into practice. A mentor will ask you the hard questions so you can live free from sin. They will help you face the daily battles in life and train you to share the gospel, serve others and make disciples as Jesus commanded us to do (Matthew 28:19-20). There's really nothing that can take the place of being discipled through a small group and by a mentor.

DEPLOYED

Saul's story shows us he wasted no time after getting rocked by Jesus. He immediately took his new faith and moved into action, something we call being deployed.

At once he began to preach in the synagogues that Jesus is the Son of God. All those who heard him were astonished and asked, "Isn't he the man who raised havoc in Jerusalem among those who call on this name? And hasn't he come here to take them as prisoners to the chief priests?" Yet Saul grew more and more powerful and baffled the Jews living in Damascus by proving that Jesus is the Messiah. (Acts 9:20-22)

For Saul, being deployed meant preaching about Jesus. God wants to deploy every one of us into our unique purpose. Like Saul, we are all called to take the message that Jesus is the Son of God into our own sphere of influence.

I love that phrase "Saul grew more and more powerful." If you have given your life to Jesus, please don't settle for anything less than this kind of growth. Never be content to coast along or let the leaders do all the ministering. Determine to stay on God's growth path and you will become more and more powerful.

In Ephesians 4, Paul tells us: "So Christ himself gave the apostles, the prophets, the evangelists, the pastors and teachers, to equip his people for works of service, so that the body of Christ may be built up" (v. 12). As leaders, we are here to equip you and others for works of service. As a pastor, I want to train people to share the gospel in their workplace, in their schools, and in their neighborhoods.

Our greatest goal as leaders is to deploy others—to send them out as missionaries into their sphere of society—the business world, the medical world, the sports world, the entertainment world, and even to other nations of the world, to share the gospel, to make disciples, and to gather people in Spirit-filled communities.

ONE STEP AT A TIME

Okay, you may be feeling a bit overwhelmed right now. Maybe you've made the decision to say yes to following Jesus but can't imagine living out all these steps. If so, I want to encourage you that faith is a journey, and no one gets there in a day or two.

But think for a minute — how will you ever know if you are becoming a mature follower of Jesus? I can promise you it doesn't come from reading enough books or going to enough church services or even attending Bible college or seminary. The only way you can be sure you are growing as a Christian is if you are getting to know Jesus more, doing the things he did and becoming more and more like Him in your character. This happens one step at a time, and all you have to do is take that next step. Have you figured out what yours is yet? The next four chapters will dig deeper into each component of the growth path.

Chapter Three

THE SECOND "D"
Dunked
(BAPTISM)

In the weeks before I popped the question to Stefanie, (who thankfully became my wife), I had the terrifying job of picking out an engagement ring. Not wanting to blow it on something so important, I asked her best friend what she might like. Evidently these conversations are the norm among young women, so she knew exactly what Stef would want—a princess cut diamond with a simple band. Yes! Let the shopping begin.

But buying the ring was the easy part. Then I had to keep it hidden and safely tucked away as we traveled to Chicago where I planned to propose. I was a nervous wreck as we went through boarding, sure TSA would make me pull it out of my jacket pocket. But I made it through and breathed a sigh of relief when I finally got to offer Stef the ring on that windy day at Lake Michigan.

The truth is that you can get engaged and even married without a ring. But let me tell you, I was so excited to walk around with Stefanie after that, knowing that she was sporting my ring and now the whole world would see that we belonged together.

This is a lot like the act of baptism. It does not save you any more than a ring makes a relationship. But if you have invited Jesus to be the Lord and Savior of your life, baptism lets the world know that you have bound your life to Him, that you and Jesus belong together! Sadly, there are a lot of Christians who have never taken this step. But do you know what Jesus did before he ever preached one sermon? That's right — He got baptized (Matthew 3:13-14).

Our English word "baptize" comes from the Greek word baptizo, which means *fully submerged*. This explains why we refer to our second "D" as *dunked*. In the Bible, just before Jesus came on the scene, there was this weird guy called "John the Baptizer" who led a revival where people got baptized to show they were repenting of their sins. He was actually preparing the way for Jesus, as he declared one day: "I baptize you with water for repentance. But after me comes one who is more powerful than I, whose sandals I am not worthy to carry. He will baptize you with the Holy Spirit and fire" (Matthew 3:11). This verse uses the imagery of being *dunked* for three different kinds of baptism. Let's talk about water baptism first, then baptism with the Holy Spirit and baptism with fire.

THE *WHAT* OF WATER BAPTISM

One day my daughter came home from school with a blue ribbon for her performance in her art class. The teachers thought her drawing was the best and gave her the ribbon to affirm her good work. A lot of people say things about baptism that make it sound like a "blue ribbon" they must earn through achievement or good behavior on their part.

This confusion comes because people don't understand the difference between religion and relationship. In religion, people try to earn their way to God, and baptism is seen as a reward for getting it right. Here are some examples of things I've heard over the years that demonstrate this faulty view:

- I don't deserve to get baptized.
- I haven't done enough or worked hard enough at my faith to get baptized.

- I don't want to get baptized because people will think I am a phony because I don't live out everything the Bible teaches.
- I'm afraid people will judge me because parts of my life don't look like a good Christian.

Can you see what's wrong with this? If baptism requires living up to some sort of religious standard, none of us will ever be qualified. A much better illustration is a birthday cake. Think about it. Why does anyone get a birthday cake? No one says, "Wow you are such a good person you should have a cake!" No, having a birthday cake happens because you were born, and people want to celebrate that.

In the same way, baptism is a celebration of your new life in Christ! You can see this in Jesus' own baptism:

As soon as Jesus was baptized, he went up out of the water. At that moment heaven was opened, and he saw the Spirit of God descending like a dove and alighting on him. And a voice from heaven said, "This is my Son, whom I love; with him I am well pleased." (Matthew 13:16-17)

God the Father watched as His Son came out of the baptismal waters and couldn't help but proclaim his love and pleasure for the world to hear. In the same way, you can be sure that when you get baptized, your heavenly Father celebrates over you with great joy. Why? Because he's given you new life, and that's worth celebrating!

In our church, as in many churches all over the world, we say a proclamation over people when we baptize them. As we put the person under water we say, "Buried with Christ in baptism," and then as they come up out of the water, we say, "and raised to walk in a new life." What we are doing is summarizing what Scripture says happened to them when they received Jesus. "If anyone is in Christ, he is a new creation. The old is gone and the new is come" (2 Corinthians 5:17).

Jesus commanded us to go into all the nations and make disciples, *baptizing them in the name of the Father and of the Son and of the Holy Spirit* (Matthew 28:19, italics added). Thus, baptism is the first act of obedience for every follower of Jesus. This is how we tell the world what Jesus has done for us. We are saying with the Apostle Paul, "I have been crucified with Christ and it is no longer I who live, but Christ who lives in me" (Galatians 2:20). That's the what of baptism. Now we'll explore the who and when by looking at a crazy Bible story about an angel, an African official and a transported preacher. You can follow along in Acts 8.

THE *WHO* OF BAPTISM

When the church was young and people like Saul were going around killing Christians, Jesus' disciples began to scatter, taking the message wherever they could. In Acts 8, we read of Philip, a radical Jesus follower who'd gone to Samaria where people flocked to hear him because when he preached, the lame and paralyzed were healed and many were delivered of evil spirits. So, he was ministering there when an angel showed up and told him to head to the desert to a road between Jerusalem and Gaza. He soon discovered that God had a divine appointment for him.

So he started out, and on his way he met an Ethiopian eunuch, an important official in charge of all the treasury of the Kandake (which means "queen of the Ethiopians"). This man had gone to Jerusalem to worship, and on his way home was sitting in his chariot reading the Book of Isaiah the prophet. The Spirit told Philip, "Go to that chariot and stay near it." (Acts 8:27-29)

Philip ran up to this African official and asked him if he understood what he was reading. The man answered that he needed someone to explain it to him and invited Philip to sit with him in the chariot. It happened that the man was reading a passage from Isaiah that prophesied Jesus' death. Talk about a perfect setup!

The eunuch asked Philip, "Tell me, please, who is the prophet talking about, himself or someone else?" Then Philip began with that very passage of Scripture and told him the good news about Jesus. As they traveled along the road, they came to some water and the eunuch said, "Look, here is water. What can stand in the way of my being baptized?" And he gave orders to stop the chariot. Then both Philip and the eunuch went down into the water and Philip baptized him. (Acts 8:26-40)

This passage tells us a lot about the *who* of baptism. The Ethiopian was hungry to know God, the only requirement needed to begin the journey of transformation. It doesn't matter what your background is. It doesn't matter whether you grew up in church or never darkened the door of one. It doesn't matter if you have a bunch of knowledge about religion or don't know the difference between a catechism and a catastrophe. What God is looking for is someone who knows their need for him.

I love this story because it levels the playing field when it comes to baptism. Do you see this? Phillip is a follower of Jesus and a Jewish man (a group that was very proud of their heritage and didn't mix with other races). But here he is, sharing the gospel with an Ethiopian, who was different from him in every way — skin color, social status, and religious background.

The point is that baptism is never limited by ethnicity or religion, and, in fact, you don't even have to be a member of a church to be baptized. Clearly, baptism is for anyone who has put their trust in Jesus to save them.

THE *WHEN* OF BAPTISM

This story makes the act of baptism so simple, it's amazing. The African official heard the good news, put his trust in Jesus, and when they came upon a pond of some sort, asked: "What can stand in the way of me being baptized?" This is the heart God wants us all to have once we've invited Jesus in. When should you get baptized? Ask yourself the question the Ethiopian asked: What can stand in the way of me being baptized?

So why do people wait? We've already talked about how religion makes you think you must earn the right or do a certain number of works to be ready for it. Unfortunately, a lot of churches have contributed to this messed up idea through the years. We made people go through a series of classes to get baptized. We made them attend a seminar. We had a required reading assignment. Often a priest or a pastor had to give his approval for someone to be baptized.

But the Bible shows how people were baptized in response to a relationship, and relationships are about grace. This is the reason we should do all that we can to help people get baptized quickly. We want to communicate clearly that just like the Ethiopian official, you don't have to do anything but *believe* in order to be baptized.

Let me tell you, you have nothing to lose and a lot to gain by choosing to get baptized. Look at the end of this story:

When they came up out of the water, the Spirit of the Lord suddenly took Philip away, and the eunuch did not see him again, but went on his way rejoicing. Philip, however, appeared at Azotus and traveled about, preaching the gospel in all the towns until he reached Caesarea. (Acts 8:39-40)

The Ethiopian was filled with joy as he went on his way—that's what God wants for you too.

BAPTISM WITH THE HOLY SPIRIT

As I've said before, I grew up in a Christian home and gave my life to Jesus at an early age. At that point, the Bible says God sealed me with His Holy Spirit (Ephesians 1:13). But I had no idea how much more of the Holy Spirit God wanted me to experience. More about that later, but first, look at the instructions Jesus gave His disciples when they were hanging out one day just before he ascended into heaven: "Do not leave Jerusalem, but wait for the gift my Father promised, which you have heard me speak about. For John baptized with water, but in a few days you will be baptized with the Holy Spirit" (Acts 1:4-5).

Missing the point completely, the disciples started asking questions, but Jesus told them all they needed to know was this: "But you will receive power when the Holy Spirit comes on you; and you will be my witnesses in Jerusalem, and in all Judea and Samaria, and to the ends of the earth" (Acts 1:8).

Do you see this? Jesus had an incredible gift for them, and it can be yours too! He wants to baptize — completely submerge – you in His

Spirit so that you will have the power to be His witness wherever you go. This came true for the disciples on the day of Pentecost when they went from being a small, timid group to bold, fiery world-changers. The most important thing about being baptized in the Holy Spirit is that it produces supernatural power to live like Jesus and proclaim His good news to people near and far.

I got rocked by this reality on my first mission trip to Mexico in college. We did street ministry and I couldn't wait to see God work through me. But no matter how I shared the gospel with people, or what I did, no one was interested. I also prayed for healing for several people, but nothing happened. It felt like a total fail.

The next morning during our worship and teaching time, our college pastor, Jimmy Siebert, spoke about the Holy Spirit and told how God was moving in power all over the world. At the end, he asked us to come forward if we were willing to humble ourselves and give God complete control so we could get more power and more of God! I practically ran down the aisle, and Jesus met me there, baptizing me in His Spirit. I literally felt his power flowing through me in a tangible way.

I can't even begin to tell you how different it was when we went to the streets that night! It seemed like everyone I talked to wanted to receive Jesus, and God even used me to bring healing to a man tormented by horrific pain.[1]

Baptism in the Holy Spirit isn't always that dramatic, but it can change your life! Here are some things to keep in mind about this experience:

- This is not a one-off, but something we can seek whenever we sense our need for more of God. In fact, the Bible tells us to continually be "filled" with the Holy Spirit (Ephesians 5:18).
- Not only can you receive more power, but God wants to give you spiritual gifts like prophecy or speaking in tongues or healing through the baptism of the Holy Spirit (Acts 19).

---

[1] You can read the entire story in my book, *The Partying God: Discovering the God of Extravagant Celebration*, Chapter Six.

- There is no one way to be baptized in the Holy Spirit — God loves variety! Read the book of Acts and you'll see how many ways God poured out His Spirit on people.
- Although you may have to wait in prayer like the disciples did before Pentecost, Jesus has promised to baptize you with His Spirit — it is part of your birthright as a believer!

So, the big question is, what do you need to do? First, while God can baptize you in His Spirit anywhere, it is helpful to go after this in community or with a trusted mentor. Second, start letting God know that you want more of him, that you are hungry for all that He will give you. Third, begin to ask God to show you anything in your life that might be blocking the Spirit's power — are there sins you are holding onto or habits you aren't willing to let Him change? And finally, simply ask! Ask the Holy Spirit to baptize you so that you can be the person He wants you to be, ready to share the good news and see people put their trust in Jesus.

BAPTISM WITH FIRE

One time as a young man, I was sitting in church listening to a message about pride versus humility, about doing what we want versus doing what God wants. Soon my skin started getting really hot, and I began to feel nauseated about my own sinfulness. In that moment, I didn't care if I humiliated myself — I just wanted to run to the altar and repent. I couldn't wait to unload all the things that were standing between God and me so that He could use me however He wanted. I didn't know it at the time, but Jesus was baptizing me with fire.

John explained the process this way: His winnowing fork is in his hand, and he will clear his threshing floor, gathering his wheat into the barn and burning up the chaff with unquenchable fire" (Matthew 3:12). What is John talking about? No, you don't have to literally be "dunked" in fire (although the disciples did have tongues of fire on their heads at Pentecost, but that's another story). Baptism with fire is a metaphor of Jesus going through our life and separating the good fruit from the sin and junk.

Being refined by fire might sound like something to dread, but it's actually a huge blessing. Sometimes we need to be set free from thoughts or behaviors that really hurt us. Other times we need to see sin as God sees it and have the kind of conviction that produces change. And sometimes God just wants to take us to a new level in our relationship with Him. Any of these things could be a catalyst for Jesus to baptize us with fire. It can take place in an instant, or over a season in your life, but baptism with fire is something we all need at different times in our spiritual journey. I encourage you to ask for it so you can be set free to experience more of Jesus in every area. Your part is simply to repent of any sins Jesus reveals—He will do the rest!

SUMMING IT ALL UP

Isn't it amazing that Jesus provides three different baptisms so we can live out our faith and receive all He has for us? What a good God! In summary:

- Baptism with water is the first act of obedience for followers of Jesus, a symbolic representation of what has happened to you. *I encourage you to get baptized as quickly as possible.*
- Baptism of the Holy Spirit is a supernatural empowering so you can be Jesus' witness wherever you go. It is usually accompanied with manifestations of joy, boldness, tongues, prophecy, and so on. *I encourage you to pray and ask God to baptize you in the Holy Spirit.* (See the prayer at end.)
- Baptism of fire is for purification to set you free and bring you a deeper walk with Jesus. *I encourage you to invite the Lord to baptize you with fire and repent of any sins He brings to mind.*

A PRAYER TO BE BAPTIZED WITH THE HOLY SPIRIT

Heavenly Father, I thank you that Jesus has saved me and that You have put Your Spirit into my heart. Now I ask for you to baptize me with the Holy Spirit according to Your Word. I open my hands and heart to receive everything you have for me — Your presence, Your anointing,

Your power and spiritual gifts. I receive this baptism by faith, believing what You have promised. Now empower me to do Your will from this day forward. Thank You, Lord Jesus, for baptizing me in Your Holy Spirit. Amen.

Chapter Four

THE THIRD "D"
Delivered

For as long as I can remember, the Herber side of my family has been known as adventurous risk-takers, forging trails where others fear to tread! That, plus the fact that I like to pride myself on being a "rugged outdoorsman," probably explains why I did what I did, landing my poor sons and me in whole lot of trouble. It started one afternoon during free time at a large ranch where we were attending a church retreat. The boys and I decided to hop in my truck and explore, and as we got to the edge of the vast property, I noticed an old unkept road heading off into nowhere. Immediately the mental debate began, like the proverbial devil on one shoulder and angel on another:

"We've got to take that and see where it leads! Adventure calls!"

"You probably shouldn't drive up that road—it clearly hasn't been used in years."

"Of course, you should take it, you're a Herber!"

"This retreat center probably doesn't want people traipsing through those unmarked areas."

"Come on, it will be fun, and no one will ever know."

"But you're out in the middle of nowhere with your three boys—it might not be that safe."

On and on it went, but in the end, my pride won out as I thought to myself: "You have been off-roading your whole life and you have a big V8 truck. You can handle this." So, we took off, and at first it was tons of fun. We barreled over rock outcroppings, winding our way through rougher and rougher territory until I finally realized that if we kept going, it was going to tear up my truck. As I pulled off the road to turn around, boom! The front left tire sunk into what seemed to be something like quicksand. I used every trick I knew to get us out, but that truck wouldn't budge.

I felt so stupid. There we were miles away from the retreat center, and no one knew where we were. My three tired and thirsty boys and I had no choice but to walk back to the lodge in the 100-degree California heat. The worst part of the whole thing was I had to tell people what I'd done because I needed their help getting my truck out of that mess. Thankfully God provided the right person, and after using a variety of tools, breaking a bunch of ropes and praying a lot, we finally got out with little damage to my truck but a lot of damage to my pride.

GETTING "UNSTUCK"

I tell that story because I want you to know that life can be like a series of those "getting stuck" moments—not in a car, but in our spiritual journeys. Whether you're a new follower of Jesus, or have been a Christian for a while, you may be stuck in some type of sin, habitual behavior or way of approaching life that is destructive to your soul. And maybe, like me with my truck, you are embarrassed or ashamed and don't really want anyone to know about your problems.

Let me just tell you that Jesus is in the business of getting people "unstuck," something the Bible often refers to as being *delivered*, which is our third "D." In fact, the Bible says: "It is for freedom that Christ has *set us free*. Stand firm, then, and do not let yourselves be burdened again by a yoke of slavery" (Galatians 5:1, italics added). Jesus wants you to know right now He died so you can be set free, that "there is now no condemnation for those who are in Christ Jesus, because through Christ Jesus the law of the Spirit who gives life has *set you free* from the law of sin and death" (Romans 8:8).

What does getting "unstuck" look like? You can have peace instead of anxiety, forgiveness and love instead of bitterness and anger, a pure heart and mind instead of lust, a satisfied soul instead of discontent. Through deliverance you can break addictions and compulsions so that the Holy Spirit controls your heart and life.

WE HAVE A REAL ENEMY

I joked earlier about a devil on my shoulder, but the truth is we have an enemy named Satan who wants to "steal, kill and destroy" everything good that Jesus wants for us (John 10:10). Every day he wanders around, looking to see who he can take down, or as the Bible says, "devour" (1 Peter 5:8). Satan would like to keep you in bondage your entire life, but his threats are empty if you've invited Jesus in as Lord:

Since therefore the children share in flesh and blood, he [Jesus] himself likewise partook of the same things, that through death he might destroy the one who has the power of death, that is, the devil, and deliver all those who through fear of death were subject to lifelong slavery. (Hebrews 2:14-15)

Do you see this? The devil wants to cripple you with fear, but Jesus has destroyed his power. Fear once made you a slave for life, but Jesus wants to deliver you from that.

Friend let me tell you, everyone in the world is stuck in some way. Everyone has someone in their lives they need to forgive. Everyone has mental strongholds they need to overcome. It's time to stop acting like we've got it all together and get real with each other so we can experience freedom!

If I haven't convinced you by now that you might need deliverance, let me throw out a few possibilities:

- Do you get irritable and hard to be around when you don't get to eat when you want?
- Do you get frustrated or anxious when you don't get enough media time (TV, movies, streaming, games, etc.)?

- Do you go shopping or buy non-essentials to make yourself feel better?
- Do you need to check your smartphone continually for posts, messages, etc., even when you are at work, in a meeting, or with a friend or family member?
- Are you unable to make it without alcohol, drugs, cigarettes, or sex?
- Do you live for social media "likes" or comments and get depressed when you don't get them?

Now you might be thinking these are just normal issues everyone deals with, and I would say: "Exactly…that's why everyone needs to be set free!" If you've *decided* to invite Jesus into your heart as Lord and Savior, and you've been *dunked* as an act of obedience to Him, your next step is to press into our third "D," *deliverance*. Your bondage to sin or harmful habits may be the result of generational strongholds from your family of origin, a temptation you've been unable to resist, or the result of your own pride, thinking you can handle things and don't need the power of God to live like Jesus. Whatever the backstory, like me with my truck, when you finally humble yourself and partner with others, you can experience complete freedom.

In this chapter you will discover three important steps to deliverance. But first, a look at someone in the Bible who blew it big-time but discovered the joy of deliverance.

A MAN NEEDING DELIVERANCE

There was this young shepherd boy who grew up to become the king of Israel and lead the nation into its golden era. He was a gifted man in the eyes of the world: a successful warrior, a prolific musician, an eloquent poet, and a winsome leader. But what strikes me most is what God said about him when he made him king: "I have found…a man after my own heart; he will do everything I want him to do" (Acts 13:22). Wow. If you haven't guessed by now, I am talking about King David.

Can you imagine having God say that about you? Most of us can't because we know how often we fail or fall into sin. But David's life is encouraging for just that reason—he was a sinful man just like we are, and God knew how far he would fall, yet he still called him a man after His own heart. What we learn from his story is that our problem is not whether we sin or how bad we blow it, but whether we know what to do to make things right and experience God's freedom.

David's storyline begins to sound like some raunchy movie when he commits adultery with Bathsheba, a woman he saw taking a bath from the roof of his palace one night. When she gets pregnant, David doesn't repent, but does what we are always tempted to do — he tries to cover it up. He takes things into his own hands, ordering her husband home from war so he will sleep with her, but when her husband doesn't do so, David has him killed (See 2 Samuel 11). Seriously?

For the next ten months David lived in a dry, almost death-like spiritual stupor. The passing pleasure of sex had pulled him into adultery and then murder without remorse. The Scriptures warn us that sin can be pleasurable, but not for long, and the outcome is always death (Hebrews 11:25, Romans 3:23). David's spiritual senses were deadened, and it seems he stopped communing with the Lord. His destiny as a "man after God's own heart" was at stake. David desperately needed deliverance.

STEP ONE: REBUKE

I am so grateful that our loving Father does not leave us in our sin but pursues us, often using another person to rebuke us. In Scripture, the Hebrew word for *rebuke* means to "reprove, correct, plea, reason or chasten." Have you ever been rebuked? Let me just tell you, this is something we all need at one time or another if we are going to walk in freedom. Jesus told us: If your brother sins, rebuke him, and if he repents, forgive him" (Luke 17:30). A wise sage in Scripture wrote: "better is open rebuke than hidden love" (Proverbs 27:5). We can so easily live in denial of where we are falling short, how we are blowing it, or the effects of habitual sin on our lives, and we need people who will love us enough to tell us what they see.

One of the first times this happened to me was when I was in high school and living a double life. I would go to church on Sundays, then go to sinful parties and mess around with girls on the weekends. One day I got a letter in the mail from a guy named Garnet. It said, in part: *"Robert, you say you are a Christian, but you live a party lifestyle like a lost person. You are living a hypocritical life."* Ouch. Rebuke is never fun, but it is often the critical first step toward freedom.

That's why God sent a prophet named Nathan to rebuke David, who began by telling the king this story:

There were two men in a certain town, one rich and the other poor. The rich man had a very large number of sheep and cattle, but the poor man had nothing except one little ewe lamb he had bought. He raised it, and it grew up with him and his children. It shared his food, drank from his cup and even slept in his arms. It was like a daughter to him. Now a traveler came to the rich man, but the rich man refrained from taking one of his own sheep or cattle to prepare a meal for the traveler who had come to him. Instead, he took the ewe lamb that belonged to the poor man and prepared it for the one who had come to him. (1 Samuel 12:1-4)

God is so gentle here — he uses a moving story that relates to David's former life as a shepherd who knew what it meant to love his sheep. How does David respond? He gets ticked off and burns with anger, demanding that whoever did this pay back four times over "because he did such a thing!" (1 Samuel 12:1-4).

This story pierced not only David's mind, but also his heart and even his physical body — he could feel God's emotions toward the injustice. What a setup! Nathan responds with: "You are the man! This is what the Lord, the God of Israel says…" (1 Samuel 12:7-9). I find this so refreshing. We are talking about David, the king who has all power and authority to destroy Nathan, yet the prophet doesn't hesitate to rebuke him because he cares more about what God says, is more concerned about God's people, and cares even more about David himself than his own life or reputation.

Friends, if you see a brother or sister in sin, lovingly confront them before they slip even further. You might be saving their life or their marriage, their job, their children, or their reputation. The Bible says that

that "whoever brings back a sinner from his wandering will save his soul from death and will cover a multitude of sins" (James 5:20). Determine right now to be willing to give and receive rebuke within your church family — your destiny or theirs may be at stake! Rebuke is a powerful gift. When it is done right, it can unleash incredible freedom.

Back to the story. Nathan went on to warn David that there would be consequences for his sin, that calamity would come to his household and everyone would see it. It is a painful truth that while God forgives, we still reap what we sow. David's sin brought pain to himself, his family, and even the nation, and he felt the consequences for the rest of his life. Yet, God still called him a man after his own heart. Why? Because of David's response. That leads us to our second step in freedom, which is *repent*.

STEP TWO: REPENT

When my boys were little, it was almost humorous when I'd see one hit the other and I'd ask: "Why did you just hit your brother?" More times than not the guilty party would respond: "I didn't!" Then I would say, "I just saw you do it," and he'd start blaming his brother or sister. It is human nature to try to cover our wrongs, to hide our sin and shift the blame. But David didn't do that in this case; he simply owned up to what he had done, saying: "I have sinned against the Lord" (1 Samuel 12: 10).

When I was a kid, we occasionally went away to stay in a little cabin out in the woods. I was always fascinated that when we turned on the lights, insects would be scurrying off into every corner. (That cabin didn't get used much!) Repentance is like that — it is as if we are turning on a light in a dark place where Satan and his demons have had free reign. Of course, your enemy wants to keep sin hidden, but when you confess, he must flee. Only then will you have the power to see what needs to change.

God's response to David's repentance was swift and amazing as Nathan assured him, "The Lord has taken away your sin. You are not going to die" (2 Samuel 1:12-13). In that moment, David was freed from the spiritual stupor he'd lived in for ten months. In a beautiful prayer in

Psalm 51, we see how David's heart changed as he took the next step in freedom, which was to *release*.

RELEASE

The first time we see Jesus in a public worship setting, he is reading these words written hundreds of years before: "He has sent me to bind up the brokenhearted, to proclaim freedom for the captives and *release from darkness for the prisoners*" (Isaiah 61:1, italics added). Jesus then shocked everyone by declaring that He was fulfilling those words that day! (Luke 4:18). Jesus came to release you from the prison of darkness that sin keeps you in. But in order to really experience that freedom, you are going to have to release — let go — of some things yourself.

LET GO OF SELF-RELIANCE

When I went on that wild ride with my boys I wrote about earlier and got my truck stuck, I was determined to get it out myself. But nothing I tried worked, and I finally had to admit that I was in a mess and needed help. I had to let go of self-reliance. I love that in Alcoholics Anonymous, this is the famous "first step" – to admit your life has become unmanageable and you are powerless to change without God.

No matter what you've done, no matter how big or small the sin or behavior is, you won't know full freedom until you humble yourself and admit you can't do this on your own. David prayed: "Have mercy on me, O God, according to your unfailing love; according to your great compassion" (Psalm 51:1). Why does David ask for mercy? Because he knows he can't fix things and he's convinced that he doesn't deserve forgiveness. So, he releases self-reliance and appeals to God's love and great compassion. He doesn't try to win God's favor or work himself back into God's presence by some gift or good work but throws himself on God's mercy.

LET GO OF SELF-JUSTIFICATION

I can't tell you how often people say, "Everyone my age is engaged in sexual sin," as if that somehow justifies it. It feels as if there is this unspoken attitude that today is different from Bible times, that some sin just can't be avoided. *Everyone cheats on their taxes, everyone watches immoral stuff on TV, everyone tells white lies to their spouse, everyone cuts corners at work* — the list goes on.

Here is what David said about his sin with Bathsheba: "For I know my transgressions, and my sin is always before me" (Psalm 51:3). David not only admits that he has sinned but also says his awareness of it never goes away. If you have been there, you know this is a miserable way to live. You literally feel that your life is marked by sin — it becomes part of your identity. And there is only one way out — to stop justifying your sin and see it for what it is.

David knew that although he'd hurt a lot of people, his sin was directly against God: "Against you, you only, have I sinned and done what is evil in your sight" (Psalm 51:4). I believe David is saying here that when he chose the path of adultery, he purposefully shut God out so he could do what he wanted. How often do we do the same thing? We ignore that inner voice of the Holy Spirit so we can continue in sin. Until we face up to what we are doing, stop blaming others or our circumstances, and stop justifying what we've done, we will not experience the deliverance Jesus has for us.

RELEASE CONTROL

When my twin sisters were two years old, they were out in a field with my parents when two horses came up and literally pushed my dad out of the way. Our small dog began to bark, and one of the horses kicked at it but hit my sister instead, breaking her jaw in seven places. Although by God's grace she survived, my sister has had physical complications from that experience her entire life. My parents never let me have a horse after that, even though I grew up on a ranch.

Fast forward to my own family. For ten years my son Hudson asked for a horse, and we finally told him to pray and prepare, and if God gave us one, we would take it. God answered, and we got a very gentle horse named Raven. I have often pondered the differences between that horse from my childhood and Hudson's horse. How does a 100-pound boy manage a 1000-pound horse? By putting a bit in its mouth and pulling on it when it goes astray so that it learns obedience. The thing about Raven was that he had been broken in so well, he didn't even need a bit anymore; he followed Hudson around like a puppy.

A big part of deliverance is letting go of control so that God can lead us with just a whisper of His voice. I don't want God to have to strong-arm me; I want to be the kind of person who listens for His gentle voice. But sometimes deliverance requires God to put that bit in our mouths and break us, so we learn obedience from the heart.

As a young man, I claimed to be following Jesus, but He wasn't really Lord in my life. Football was my idol, and selfishness was my character. I would put others down to be popular, I stole my best friend's girlfriend, and I had begun to slip into sexual sin. Then, boom! I was laid out with a serious heart problem that changed everything. I'm not saying God sent that affliction, but I know He used it to break me so that I would release control of my life.

David experienced such brokenness through his sin, praying: "Let me hear joy and gladness; let the bones you have crushed rejoice" (Psalm 51:8). However God may choose to break you, your path to freedom must include a decision to give Him control of everything in your life. God heard my cries through that painful season and healed me, and that is the reason I am here dreaming God's dreams instead of my own today, which leads to our final step in deliverance, *restoration*.

RESTORATION

Anytime I have spiraled into sin, I've known that God didn't abandon me, but I lost the sweetness of his fellowship. I lost my joy and the peace of walking closely with him. I no longer felt the tender touch of God's presence. And I would miss it so much. But I have found over and over that as I repent and release control back to Him, He restores me with His presence and fills me with joy.

David prayed, "Restore to me the joy of your salvation and grant me a willing spirit, to sustain me" (Psalm 51:12). We know we've been restored when our joy returns. If you have lost your joy as a follower of

Jesus, take some time to check your life — you may need some deliverance. It could be anything — idolatry, selfishness, greed, comparison, discontent — all of these and more can steal your joy.

What does restoration look like? The story of David rocks me every time I think of how kind God is. The backstory is that David ended up marrying Bathsheba, and she gave birth to another son — Solomon, one of the wisest men who ever lived. He became king after David and was used by God to build the Temple (1 Samuel 13). This is crazy. After repenting and releasing, David prayed for *restoration*, and God responds by blessing a marriage that had begun in sin. God even goes on to use Bathsheba powerfully in David and Solomon's lives.

Do you know that God is kinder than we can ever imagine? When He delivers us, though we still experience the consequences of our sin, God brings blessing out of everything, even our disobedience. Friend, no matter how much you've blown it or how bad your situation is — restoration is possible! You can be set free to live in God's favor from this moment forward!

DELIVERANCE PRAYER

I suffered from headaches from childhood until I was a young man, and nothing seemed to help. Then one time I was at a missions team meeting and my head started hurting, so I asked for prayer. As they were praying, a woman asked a question about family members who might have been involved in organizations that use occultic practices. I told her one possibility, and she explained how men in that organization made spiritual vows that opened the door to Satan, though most didn't know it. I immediately repented for myself and my family, asked Jesus to heal me, and commanded evil spirits to leave. Immediately those headaches went away and have never come back!

Most of this chapter has been about deliverance and the steps we need to take when we have sinned. But there are times when Satan and his demons are oppressing you and you need another step — freedom prayer. There are a lot of ways demons gain access — from alcohol, to drugs, to evil movies, to involvement with the occult, to bitterness and unforgiveness, to generational sin, to painful childhood experiences. It might not be anything you have done, but what was done to you.

How do you know if you are oppressed? You might feel something physical, like being pressed down on your bed or choked at night or feeling like something has taken control over you. It might be mental — having accusing voices in your head or feeling like something is telling you to end your life. These are just a few of the common ways, and whenever I talk about this, people always come up to me afterwards and say, "Pastor that is me. That is what I was dealing with."

Jesus is able to deliver anyone! He spent a lot of time on earth setting people free from demonic oppression, and then he commanded his disciples to cast out demons. This should be a normal part of our lives and ministry. At our church, we offer an entire day of teaching and prayer so that people can be delivered. We call it "Freedom Day" because we believe every follower of Jesus has the right to live in freedom!

JESUS IS OUR TRUE SOURCE OF FREEDOM

I want to end this chapter with a verse that is so encouraging from the book of Acts. It says: "Jesus went around doing good and healing all who were under the power of the devil" (Acts 10:38). This is incredible. Jesus wants to do good to you and not harm. He does not condemn or shame you, but he meets you in your sickness, your pain, your sorrow and your sin so He can heal, love, restore and deliver you.

The third "D" – *deliverance* – is possible because of Jesus. He wants you free from sin and Satan's oppression more than you can ever imagine. Why? He wants to walk with you, to be Your friend and guide, and to fill your life with His wonderful presence so that you can live out His dreams and purposes with peace and joy. Setting people free is what Jesus does, it is who He is, and it is why He died on the cross. Deliverance is your birthright as His follower!

You can experience this freedom today. Below is a two-part process to ask Jesus for deliverance. You can pray it right now or ask a mentor or small group to pray with you and for you as you go through it.

Part 1: *Father, I thank you that the death, resurrection and ascension of Jesus sets me free from all demonic affliction and oppression. I claim the power of the blood of Jesus Christ over my life. I now command every spirit to leave me and go back to the pit of hell.*

Part 2: *I repent of partnering with the spirit of _____ (Be specific in naming any spirit that has afflicted you. This might include things like a suicidal spirit, lustful spirit, violent spirit, mental tormenting spirit, etc.). I confess that I have sinned (specifically name any sin that is coming to mind), and I now turn away from that sin. I command this spirit to leave me now in the name of Jesus. I ask the Holy Spirit to fill me and any place that sin or demonic spirits have had access in my life.*

(Take a moment to breathe in deeply letting the Holy Spirit fill you. Then repeat Part 2 as many times as God brings different evil spirits to mind that he is wanting to free you from.)

The Scriptures tell us: "It is for freedom that Christ has set us free. Stand firm, then, and do not let yourselves be burdened again by a yoke of slavery" (Galatians 5:14). You can move forward with strength and confidence, standing firm because you know that Jesus has delivered you.

Chapter Five

THE FOURTH "D"
Discipled

From as early as I can remember, I was drawn to nature and wanted to be a true outdoorsman. I watched National Geographic and other travel shows and longed to be like those people with hiking backpacks who trekked miles into the wilderness to camp in pristine, wild settings. My Dad was a hunter and fisherman, but he had bad allergies and limited time, plus we lived in the center of Texas where there were no national parks, so I never had the chance to fulfill those dreams. Beyond that, the fact that I knew nothing about where to go, what to pack, or how to feed myself made me more than a little scared to explore the wilderness by myself.

Then I met my college roommate who was a backpacker extraordinaire. Coming from Little Rock, Arkansas, Robert Fuller had logged countless hours exploring the beautiful Ozark mountain chain. He often reminisced longingly of those adventures, cooking up scrumptious meals in an iron skillet over an open fire, pitching his tent dozens of miles from the nearest person, and staring up into a night sky that was unblemished by city light pollution. I wanted that kind of adventure so badly that one day I asked if he would take me.

He happily agreed, and we made a plan to go hiking as soon as school got out. Meanwhile, he began to prepare me. He taught me about gear — real hiking boots that could withstand the weight of the inner frame backpack I'd need in order to carry my sleeping bag, small tent and other gear. As we planned and prepared, I was more than a little nervous, so on our first day, Fuller took me on a several-hour climb up Pinnacle mountain just outside of the city. Feeling a sense of accomplishment as we got to the top and looked at the beautiful view, I couldn't wait for the real hike.

It was an amazing time as Fuller taught me to do things that I had always wanted to do, like prepare meals over a campfire or follow a guidebook to all kinds of beautiful vistas and discoveries far off the trail of amateur tourists. He actually took me spelunking, an exhilarating endeavor I could never have done on my own. We trekked into those dark caverns with both headlamps and spare flashlights, following the instructions that more experienced spelunkers had previously taught Fuller. I can't even begin to tell you what it was like entering that massive underground arena. What an incredible adventure. I came back so stoked and confident that someday I would pass what I'd learned down to my own kids.

Over the years I have often heard people talk longingly about dreams they had, adventures they wanted to take, or hobbies they wanted to delve into, but then bemoan the fact that they never had anyone to teach them how. The truth is, we learn best as human beings when we have someone else mentor us along. Jesus knew this and spent his adult life mentoring others. Do you know why? Because every human being has an innate desire for an authentic friendship with God but needs someone to show them how. Jesus came to earth and did this perfectly through a process he called *making disciples*, which leads us to our fourth "D" — *discipled*.

You don't have to look any further than Jesus' final words to His followers as He was about to ascend into heaven to know that making disciples was uppermost in His heart and mind:

Then Jesus came to them and said, "All authority in heaven and on earth has been given to me. Therefore, go and make disciples of all nations, baptizing them in the name of the Father and of the Son and of the Holy Spirit, and teaching them to obey everything I have commanded you. And surely I am with you always, to the very end of the age. (Matthew 28:18- 20)

It's pretty clear to me that Jesus intended for the people He'd been teaching, leading and mentoring to turn around and do the same thing for others. This has been God's plan now for over two thousand years, and it still works! Not only can you have the blessing of being discipled once you've decided to follow Jesus, but you also then get the privilege of passing on what you have received by *discipling* others. More about that later, but first, let's look at how Jesus discipled, since he is our model.

JESUS, THE CHURCH PLANTER

We live in a time when we rarely we get through a day without hearing about some demoralizing event — a terrorist attack killing scores of innocent people, the latest school shooting, another horrific act of racism or some sickening case of domestic violence, to name a few. Bad news screams at us from our phones and TVs, and we can sometimes wonder if there is any safe place for us or any place where good overcomes evil.

I find such encouragement in Jesus' words: "I will build my church and the gates of hell will not prevail against it!" (Matthew 16:18). The Son of God established one institution while he was on earth, and it was the church, which he endowed with power to overcome the evil ploys of hell. Unfortunately, a lot of people have a very skewed idea of what the church is. If you didn't grow up in a church, your main exposure to it may have been in movies that depict it as a small building with a cross on top and long benches called pews where people come to listen to a priest or preacher. In other words, church is boring, antiquated and a little hokey.

Even many Christians think of church as a Sunday service, which is way too narrow for what Jesus intended. In fact, the word He used in that verse above is the Greek word ekklesia, which literally means "called out ones." What are we called out from? The pain, the selfishness, the hedonism and destructive patterns of the world. What are we called to? To be a family who will hear Jesus' voice and go on a journey of faith together, being filled with the Holy Spirit so we can overcome the world.

Now this may surprise you: if you want to know what a church is to be, look no further than Jesus and closest His band of followers! Jesus was the first church planter! Although He did draw large crowds at times, Jesus spent most of His time focused on training the *ekklesia* or called-out ones. This included a very targeted group of twelve men, with a more intentional focus on three of them. For Jesus, discipleship was the church!

DISCIPLESHIP THROUGH SMALL GROUPS

Years ago, I heard of a very sad phenomenon taking place in Russia. Orphanages had been inundated with babies, and researchers were called in because the little ones were dying, and they couldn't find a cause. The specialists found that the conditions were sanitary, the children were being provided healthy hygiene, and they were given sufficient food. However, the orphanages were understaffed and over-crowded, and the workers had no time for extra care such as holding the children, talking to them, rocking them to sleep, or calling them by name — all the things that should happen in a normal, healthy home. The result was a lack of physical and emotional development, with many young ones simply giving up the will to live.[2]

As human beings, we have an innate need for love and nurture, and this is especially true in our spiritual lives. We simply cannot make it on our own, nor did Jesus ever intend for us to. When you decide to invite Jesus into your life, the Holy Spirit within makes you want to learn how to pray, how to understand the Bible, how to shape your life into one that is pleasing to the Lord, and how to share your faith with your friends and

---

[2] Early research showed that 1/3 of neglected babies in these understaffed orphanages died, while half of the rest developed severe mental illness. See https://www.huffpost.com/entry/how-orphanages-kill-babie_b_549608 for example.

family. Small groups are the place where fellow believers who love you and love Jesus can nurture and mentor you. As a pastor I have had a front row seat to watch people from all different backgrounds with different challenges and pains come into God's family to find love, belonging and ultimately transformation through a small group.

Sociologists and psychologists say that the number twelve is significant because it is about the number of people who can have authentic relationships in a room where everyone is known and can share their opinions, thoughts and heart. Time after time in Scripture we see Jesus walking with his group of twelve, eating meals together, engaging in deep conversations and modeling some kind of kingdom value or behavior.

In the early church, we see a similar pattern. After Jesus ascended and the Holy Spirit baptized His followers in power on Pentecost, 3000 people made decisions to follow Him at a huge outdoor service. So how did that band of original disciples train and care for all of those folks? We find the answer in Acts:

> *They devoted themselves to the apostles' teaching and to fellowship, to the breaking of bread and to prayer. Everyone was filled with awe at the many wonders and signs performed by the apostles. All the believers were together and had everything in common. They sold property and possessions to give to anyone who had need. Every day they continued to meet together in the Temple courts. They broke bread in their homes and ate together with glad and sincere hearts, praising God and enjoying the favor of all the people. And the Lord added to their number daily those who were being saved. (Acts 2:42-47)*

So apparently, the original church had large gatherings, but they also they met in small groups from house to house, and this passage tells us exactly what they were doing. Small groups are one of the ways ongoing discipleship takes place in the church Jesus established — just as He modeled for us while He lived in the earth. If you are ready for our fourth "D" – *discipled*, in your journey, a small group is a great place to begin.

Let me just tell you though, that it isn't enough to spend time with other believers — riding bikes, watching sports together, surfing together, having kids play dates together, etc. These are all great — do them, but make sure you are in a group that can disciple you by including the powerful elements the book of Acts describes so that transformation takes place. Let's briefly summarize these.

They Devoted Themselves: When I first encountered the presence and power of Jesus, I visited church after church, looking for people that were on fire for Him, but to my dismay, it seemed like most people went to church on Sundays and for the next six days lived no differently from anyone else. It took me three years, but I finally found some people who were radical for Jesus and wanted Him to influence every aspect of their lives. They met in small groups and let me tell you, they were *devoted*. This is what I believe God wants — a devoted church who follow Jesus wholeheartedly.

To the Apostles Teaching: It is amazing that you and I can listen to sermons any hour of the day, from the best teachers and preachers in Christianity. Although that is a huge blessing, I have to say there is a big difference between being a connoisseur of sermons and being devoted to the Bible's teaching. The early church was devoted to applying what they learned. They understood that a true disciple was not just a hearer of the Word, but a doer. Small groups are the place where you can unpack the Scriptures with others and learn how to appropriate what you've learned as you go throughout the rest of the week.

To Fellowship: In the early days when cell phones first came out, I remember going to lunch and seeing four men sitting together eating, but every one of them was on their phone. I thought that was the craziest thing I'd ever seen, but now it's the norm! People interact far more with their smartphones than other human beings around them. Having face to face conversations and learning to express emotions verbally is a lost art. Relationships seem to be more about convenience than friendship.

I want you to know that there is nothing like a small group to "refamily" someone. More and more people are growing up without the basic tools of engagement with others. In small group discipleship, you learn how to communicate with people, how to care for them, how to have healthy interactions and understand their hearts. Small groups are all about people — a place to feel needed and learn life together.

Breaking Bread Together: We may do a lot of things with a lot of people, but when we sit down to eat, it is usually with those we feel close to. Few things in life build friendship more than eating a meal together. There is just something about sitting down at the table that is so disarming and enjoyable. Jesus modeled this a lot — He was always eating with people in order to pursue a relationship with them. Eating with others in your small group will disciple you in ways worship or study can't. It is an important part of the process.

In Scripture, breaking bread also refers to the act of communion, which is another aspect of life together in small groups. As you take the time to remember and reflect on the Gospel — Jesus' death and resurrection, you are bonded together over what matters most in the family of God. Practicing this often is a valuable way for the Gospel to take root deep within you.

Prayer: As a teenager I remember a holiday meal when one of my uncles asked me to pray. I stuttered and stammered so much that another uncle came up to me and said, "You need to work on that — you just kept saying 'uh.'" At first, I was offended and thought he had no right to judge my prayer. But then I realized, I really didn't know how to pray. I don't know about you, but I feel like prayer is one of the most intimidating aspects of being a Christian. Most people feel like they don't really know how to pray, and the idea of praying out loud is terrifying.

This is where small groups are so great because they give you the chance to practice an important part of following Jesus. You will quickly learn that the more you do it, the more you'll feel like you are just talking with God, and it gets easier. Then when you see God answer prayer, you will be amazed, and your confidence will increase until you become hooked on prayer!

Signs and Wonders: One reason a lot of people are not interested in church is because they don't see any power, and it feels like an outdated social club. The early church taught us that miracles should be taking place regularly, for this is what sets us apart from every other institution. Jesus promised that whenever two or more people gather in His name, He is there! This means that through His Spirit, Jesus will come and do signs and wonders through each and every person there. This is one of the greatest joys you will know as a disciple of Jesus.

Everything in common: The American culture teaches us to take care of ourselves first and foremost, and then maybe our families. But Jesus showed us a different way where people learn to meet the needs of those around them, to care for their brothers and sisters, their new spiritual family. When you are discipled in a small group, you learn how to live like Jesus in selfless giving.

Added to their number: When something is lifegiving, it cannot help but grow. This was true of the early church and will be true of small groups today who live as disciples of Jesus. The great thing about being discipled in a small group is that it gives you a place to bring friends and family, to show them how the life of Jesus is demonstrated in the relationships there.

I hope you have a good picture of how you can be discipled by joining a small group. Don't wait another day to align yourself with a group of Jesus' followers who practice the things I've listed above and let them into your life so they can disciple you. I will just add here, if you have been a member of a small group for some time, God may be calling you to lead a small group. Jesus is about us expanding our borders by discipling others as we have been discipled, and this is a great opportunity for many of you to take that next step.

DISCIPLESHIP MENTORING

So far, we've been talking about discipleship in small groups, as Jesus discipled his band of 12. But Jesus also homed in on three of those men, spending more focused time with them. The moment you accept Jesus into your heart, you are ready for this kind of relationship. As great as small groups are, they can only take you so far in your journey. Just like I needed an experienced hiker to show me how, you need someone who is passionate about Jesus to show you how to walk with Him.

When I was in college I wanted so badly to grow in my faith. I went to as many Christian activities as I could. I went to big rallies, I belonged to a traveling music group, and I was part of a Christian leadership organization, but when I watched my roommate's life, I knew I wasn't growing like he was. The difference was he was being discipled by a guy named Mark. Now let me be honest, the first time I met Mark I wasn't overwhelmingly impressed. He just seemed like a nice, normal guy. But I'll never forget him explaining: "I'm here because I believe revival is going to break out on campus." I thought to myself, "No one who has the time to hang out in some other guy's apartment is going to start a revival." Then he said this: "My strategy is to meet with a couple of guys and disciple them."

Now if you'd have asked me how to bring a revival, I would have said we needed to get a huge crowd, have great music, smoke, lights, t-shirts—whatever was in at the time. But I watched Mark meet with my roommate week after week and he was getting rocked! I felt this longing inside of me, and I wanted to know how this guy trained people like my roommate.

One of the things I was excited about when I went on my first mission trip to Mexico was getting to be around Mark. I watched how he encouraged people, how he was always sharing the gospel with people, and how wise he was in different situations. After we returned home, I asked him if he would disciple me. He said he'd pray about it, and the next time we met, he challenged me to spend my life making disciples, to invest my college years in a few guys at a time. If I was willing to do that, then he was willing to disciple me.

You see, part of being discipled is to understand that every follower of Jesus is called to make disciples—even you! I'll explain more later, but first let me share the three things Mark drilled into me week after week that are the pillars of any mentoring discipleship. I call them *Look Up, Look In,* and *Look Out*, and they make the process so simple, anyone can do it.

LOOK UP

The very first week I moved to San Diego from Texas, I asked a surfer if he'd teach me to surf. His name was Tommy, and when I showed up at his house in Ocean Beach, he first showed me how to get down on the floor and pop up. He modeled it, and then he made me try it a bunch of times. Then we got to the beach and he told me to follow him into the water with my board. Battling the winter swell, I finally caught up with him and again, he told me to watch him as a wave came. He paddled furiously, then popped up, rode the wave, and then swam back and told me to try it. I think I only caught one wave that day, and I was so sore I had to soak in a hot bath for half an hour, but I could then claim I had surfed because Tommy had modeled for me.

This is exactly how Jesus trained his followers to look up – by modeling it for them. As a college student I really wondered if I could be close to God— was it even possible? Even though I'd grown up in the church, I didn't feel like I really knew Him. But that is exactly why Jesus came to earth—to show us how to have a relationship with God. And it all begins by looking up through prayer. Jesus' life was marked by prayer—He modeled it so well that the disciples asked him to teach them how:

> *One day Jesus was praying in a certain place. When he finished, one of his disciples said to him, "Lord, teach us to pray, just as John taught his disciples." He said to them, "When you pray, say: 'Father, hallowed be your name, your kingdom come.... Give us each day our daily bread. Forgive us our sins, for we also forgive everyone who sins against us. And lead us not into temptation.'"*
> *(Luke 11:1-4)*

Jesus showed His disciples how to pray by praying in front of them.

But Jesus didn't just model prayer, he explained how to do it, saying, "When you pray," and then He unpacked a paradigm for prayer that still works.

- "Our Father": Looking up for intimacy
- "Hallowed be your name": Looking up through worship

- "Your kingdom come": Looking up through intercession (praying for others)
- "Give us this day our daily bread": Looking up through petition (praying for our own needs)
- "Forgive us our sins": Looking up through repentance
- "Lead us not into temptation but deliver us from evil": Looking up for protection

Mark did a similar thing for me the first time we met, explaining that *looking up* would be our first priority. He had me put on a song so we could worship, then he explained who we were going to pray for, and how — from those in our small group to those who didn't know Jesus. Mark would pray, then he'd have me pray. I know my prayer life is strong today because he taught, modeled and then had me practice.

Mark also showed me how to study the Bible. The Bible is an amazing book that God has given us so that we can experience His presence, understand His ways and discover His will for our daily lives. While it was written over 1500 years by around 40 different people, it really tells one grand story of who God is, why He created the world, and how much He loves human beings. The Bible is the most important book you'll ever own as a follower of Jesus because it is all about Him.

Every word in Scripture is inspired by God — no other book can make such a claim! That's why it is good for "teaching, rebuking, correcting and training in righteousness" (2 Timothy 3:16). There are lots of ways to read the Bible, but here is how Mark taught me. We would read some verses with a pen and paper in hand, then he would have us write down our thoughts on what we were learning, as well as any questions we had. It wasn't long before I learned how to really focus on God's Word and apply it to my life.

Mark also taught me how to hear God's voice. First, he explained by showing me Scriptures about hearing God, and then he helped me practice waiting silently before the Lord and journaling what I thought I'd heard. Through all these things I learned that Scripture and prayer are the foundation for following Jesus and everything else has to flow from this time with Him. Daily time in prayer with Jesus has remained the most stabilizing factor in my life. In discipleship mentoring, you get to have someone model not only these things, but all sorts of spiritual practices so that you can then try them on your own.

LOOK IN

The second important component in any discipleship is *looking in* — learning to be honest about our lives and asking each other questions to help pinpoint where we might be struggling. Mark and I had a list of questions we went through — from questions about my thought life to how I treated my family to how I'd shared (or failed to share) my faith in the past week. The point is that discipleship is meant to transform our lives, and we have to learn to be vulnerable and real with each other for that to happen. I never felt condemned when Mark asked me those questions, and just knowing he would ask made me want to live with a pure heart and radical obedience to Jesus. Looking in relies on an accountability every one of us needs in order to grow in our faith and is an important part of discipleship.

LOOK OUT

Finally, every discipling relationship must include *looking out* to the world around us. I grew up hearing sermons on sharing the Gospel and heard often how important it was that I be a bold witness for Jesus. But I didn't learn how until I began to hang out with Mark and he modeled it for me. Everywhere we went, he struck up friendly conversations that at some point turned to his faith. He wasn't forceful or preachy but shared with kindness and an honest interest in the lives of the people we met.

Mark also modeled serving others as a lifestyle. He would take me along when he went to help fix someone's car or brought food to the homeless. When we hung out together, he just naturally looked for ways to help others. I learned from watching him and ministering with him that true leadership was about being a servant.

This is only a portion of what I learned from Mark, but the reverberating effects of him discipling me will continue through eternity. Let me just tell you that there is only one thing you can invest in that will last forever, and that is people. Discipleship is a way to invest in people. This is probably the most important thing Mark modeled for me, and since those college years I have had the privilege of discipling hundreds of men.

I often hear people say they want a church with "deeper teaching," that they want to hear about the mature things in our faith and aren't interested in the basics anymore. Now, I am all for that — I study original languages, I'm a student of ecclesiology and eschatology, but what I learned from Mark is that true spiritual maturity is actually *doing* the Word of God.

So, let me ask you: Do you make disciples? Do you spend daily time with Jesus? Do you ask others to hold you accountable in your thoughts and actions? Do you share your faith? In other words, do you live looking up, looking in and looking out? True biblical maturity means living like Jesus and helping others do the same.

DISCIPLES WHO MAKE DISCIPLES

As a pastor, I am relentless in calling people not only to be discipled, but to go out and make disciples. Why? There are a lot of great reasons — it will help you grow in your faith, you'll be investing in eternity, and it's really fun! But do you know what drives me day in and day out when it comes to making disciples? The motivation that keeps me going and the one that matters most of all? Simply put, I make disciples because Jesus said to. Remember His final words to the disciples? Go therefore into all the world and *make* disciples (Matthew 28:20).

This is it. I have discipled other people since I was 20 years old because Jesus said to, and for me, disobedience is not an option. You just have to decide in life — is your goal to obey Jesus? He didn't say you have to be great at making disciples, He didn't say you have to love it, He didn't say how many disciples you have to make. But He did say to you and to me and to everyone who claims to be His follower: Go and make disciples.

Now you may be feeling a little intimidated, thinking, "I'm not like Jesus; he was perfect. I could never disciple someone. I am sinful and

I've made so many mistakes." Can I tell you that Jesus isn't looking for perfect people, He is looking for available people! Making disciples is not for the spiritually elite. It is not for the few, it is not for authors of books, it is not for the seminary trained, or the super saints. Making disciples is for every believer.

Sure, we can all look at our lives and see major flaws and feel totally inadequate to make disciples. But think about the disciple-makers in Scripture: Paul was a murderer, Peter was a loud-mouth who denied Jesus, John was a hot head and prideful position-seeker, Thomas was a doubter, yet where would the church be today if they hadn't obeyed Jesus' command?

Let me assure you — you *can* make disciples! I am not saying it is easy; in fact it can be hard and that's why a lot of people don't do it. They'd rather sit in classes or read books or listen to podcasts or bounce around from this church to that, looking for the best worship experience. But let me just say you have nothing to lose and everything to gain!

It is a tried and true spiritual principle that when you pour yourself into others, God will pour blessings you can't even imagine into your lap. Jesus promised: "Give, and it will be given to you. A good measure, pressed down, shaken together and running over, will be poured into your lap. For with the measure you use, it will be measured to you" (Luke 6:38). The more you give yourself away, the more you will experience all that Jesus has for you. In fact, Philemon 1:6 says: "I pray that you may be active in sharing your faith, so that you will have a full understanding of every good thing we have in Christ." Do you see this? Sharing your faith with others is the key to understanding and experiencing all the good things God has for you.

Think about it — every other relationship, whether focused on sports or school or work or whatever, is going to end in one way or another. But when you invest in discipleship mentoring, you are investing in kingdom relationships that will last for eternity. I can honestly say that the deepest friendships I have are those that have invested in me or I've invested in them through discipleship.

Friends, there is nothing like the joy of seeing the people you've discipled grow in Christ. The Apostle John walked personally with Jesus, saw the Holy Spirit poured out at Pentecost and helped usher in the explosive growth of the early church, but in his old age, he wrote this: "I have no greater joy than to hear that my children are walking in the truth" (3 John 1:4). No greater joy! That's discipleship.

So, if this is your next step, don't waste any time. Ask someone to disciple you today! If they don't have time or turn you down for some reason, ask someone else and keep asking until you find someone who will. Then, as soon you can, find someone else that you can pour your life into. Go therefore and make disciples! An old preacher used to say: "God said it, I believe it, that settles it!" But can I just add one thing?

Go therefore and make disciples!

God said it. You believe it. That settles it.

Now go do it!

Chapter Six

THE FIFTH "D"
Deployed

A while back we were at a beach birthday party for a friend. The adults were sitting around sharing stories and playing instruments, and the kids were running around in the sand when a friend realized his three-year-old daughter wasn't nearby. We all started looking and calling out her name while her father ran to the water and waded in, hoping against hope that she hadn't gotten sucked under a wave. In sheer panic we spread out — some to the parking lot, some to the restrooms, others asking everyone on the beach if they'd seen her. Several minutes passed and she was nowhere to be found.

At some point I noticed a large sand dune and decided to climb it to get a better vantage point. When I reached the top, I saw a tiny speck about three football fields away. I had no idea if that was her, but I took off running as fast as I could. As I drew near, I was so relieved to see it was my friend's daughter, crying hysterically. The poor thing was so vulnerable and helpless— I just cannot tell you what it felt like to sweep her up in my arms and tell her everything was going to be okay. I ran back to my friend, who saw me from a distance and took off toward us. When I placed his precious daughter in his arms, my friend responded with tremendous emotion, expressing his thankfulness again and again. What a privilege it was to bring back a lost child to the arms of her loving father.

As I begin this chapter on our final "D" – *deployed* – this story is on my heart because it is such a beautiful picture of the privilege each of us have as followers of Jesus. Do you realize you are called to go out, find the lost children and put them back into our Heavenly Father's arms? To me, there is no greater honor, no higher privilege and nothing more rewarding than this. What could possibly compare to knowing you get to be a part of healing God's heart that is broken for our lost world?

The Bible says that Jesus came "to seek and to save that which was lost" (Luke 19:10 AMP). This was His mission, and His message was clear and simple: "The time has come.". "The kingdom of God has come near. Repent and believe the good news!" When God's kingdom is near, not only are lost children brought home to experience His reign in their lives, but heaven comes to earth and amazing things happen. Because God is good and perfect, His kingdom is the best news any person, family, culture, society or nation can experience! Jesus taught this, modeled it, and sent His followers out to do the very things He did to bring His kingdom, saying: "As the Father has sent me, I am sending you" (John 20:21). Are you ready for this? From the moment you decided to invite Jesus into your heart, you were deployed, whether you knew it or not!

EVERYBODY GETS TO PLAY

I loved sports growing up, but in junior high I had an accident that ended my football career and put me in and out of the hospital for a whole year. By God's grace I was eventually supernaturally healed, but by the time I could play sports again, I was in college and had fallen way behind my peers because of lack of practice. I was terribly disappointed when I wasn't asked to be on the intramural football team because I hadn't played football in high school. I envied the comradery of all these other guys as they shared the excitement of the battle and the joy of victory. As a former athlete, this was painful and emotionally challenging.

It is no fun to sit on the sidelines, in sports and in life. We've all experienced the hurt of not being invited in, of feeling left out or being picked last, as if we had nothing to offer. But God's heart is to draw each one of us in, to give every person who is willing a part to play in His purposes for the world. God has no favorites and doesn't want to leave anyone on the sidelines.

A lot of people think only Jesus' twelve disciples were on mission, but that is not true. Jesus deployed His whole church, beginning with the twelve:

And he called the twelve together, and gave them power and authority over all demons, and to cure diseases. And he sent them forth to preach the kingdom of God, and to heal the sick. ... And they departed, and went throughout the villages, preaching the gospel, and healing everywhere. (Luke 9:1-2, 6)

Then He brought in a group of 72:

After this the Lord appointed seventy-two others and sent them two by two ahead of him to every town and place where he was about to go. He told them, "...Heal the sick who are there and tell them, 'The kingdom of God has come near to you.'" (Luke 10:1, 9)

And just to make it clear that Jesus has a place for you, look at what He prayed at the end of His life:

As you sent me into the world, I have sent them into the world.... My prayer is not for them alone. I pray also for those who will believe in me through their message." (John 17:18-20)

How incredible is it that Jesus prayed for you and me, affirming that He was sending us into the world in the same way His Father sent Him? You are called, commissioned, and sent forth to bring the kingdom near wherever you go every day of your life! Jesus has deployed you! Now you might be thinking: "Me? I'm not a preacher" or "I work in an office" or "I stay home and take care of my children" or "I'm just a student" so how can I be deployed? Let me just tell you that no matter what your life circumstances, if you have made a decision to invite Jesus into your life, He has a mission for you. Everybody gets to play!

OCCUPATION VERSUS VOCATION

"What are you going to be when you grow up?" is a question that adults ask kids, and kids ask each other all the time. I remember for the longest time telling people I wanted to be the President of the United States. Then I wanted to be a Disney animator. Then I wanted to be an actor in movies. In college I stressed out when they asked me to declare a major because I felt like I was being forced to choose what I would be, and I still wasn't sure. That is probably why I changed majors four times!

But then God clearly called me to be a pastor, and I got really focused on that. I started to daydream about it, determining to get as much education as I could so I would have tons of letters after my name. I wanted to be Pastor Herber, Rev. Herber, Dr. Herber, Robert Herber, PhD. I thought if I could get as many degrees as possible, I'd impress people and look like I had an important job. Then one day, just when I was positive that I was about to get a pastoral position at a church, I had a meeting with my pastor, who told me I wasn't ready. Although I know now how right he was, at the time I felt devastated and deeply disappointed.

The next day as I walked and talked with God, I felt Him saying He wanted to give me a life vision statement. I was excited and waited expectantly for something profound. The first thing I heard was: "Robert I want you to love Jesus." And I thought, boy that is simple, but it is Biblical too, and I thought of the verse that says to love God "with all your heart, with all your understanding and with all your strength" (Mark 12:33). Then I said, "God, is there anything else?" and immediately the phrase "feed my sheep" came to mind. I thought, that is Biblical too as I remembered in John 21:15 where Jesus said to Peter "if you love me, feed my sheep." I felt like that was still really simple, so I asked again, "God, is there anything else?" And immediately the phrase came, "fish for men." I remembered Mark 1:17 where Jesus told his disciples to come and follow him and he'd make them fishers of men.

What came next was truly profound. I felt like God said, "Robert, no matter what vocation you have in life, whether you are a pastor or work behind the counter at the corner store, whether you are a doctor or a garbage man, no matter what you are doing, if you do these three

things—love Jesus, feed my sheep and fish for men—you will be incredibly successful in my kingdom.
- Love Jesus (God) Mark 12:330
- Feed his sheep John 21:15
- Fish for men Mark 1:17

These three things became the foundation of my life. Every day I invest time in my relationship with Jesus. Every day I try to make disciples and care for Jesus' followers, and every day I look for the lost around me and for opportunities to bring them the gospel. This can all be summarized as building God's kingdom.

The important lesson I learned that day was that my occupation was far more important than my vocation. The dictionary defines occupation as "the principle business of one's life." Let me just say that Jesus does not want any job, whether it's waiting tables or computer programming or managing an office, to be the principle business of your life. He told us what he wants it to be in Matthew 6:33: *"But seek first his kingdom and his righteousness, and all these things will be given to you as well."* You see, we all have the same occupation — to build God's kingdom in every area of our lives, wherever we go.

On the other hand, the dictionary defines *vocation* as "a summons or strong inclination to a particular state or course of action." In His brilliance, God deploys each of us to build His kingdom in unique ways across every sector of society through our different vocations. In Jesus' initial group of followers, there were fishermen, doctors, accountants, wealthy society women and historians, to name a few.

Look at the variety in the early church alone:
- Paul was a tentmaker, along with Priscilla and Aquilla
- Cornelius was a military officer
- Simon was a tanner
- Onesimus was a household servant
- Dorcas was a clothing designer

All of these played an important part in spreading the gospel and establishing God's kingdom.

So, whatever your vocation might be, I want to encourage you that Jesus has a plan for you to fulfill His call, and you don't have to be a pastor or an overseas missionary to do it (although He might call you to that too!). The question isn't whether you have been deployed, but what you have been deployed to do in your situation. We are going to see that all of us are deployed to do what Jesus did, to get the gospel to the ends of the earth, and to active duty in a wartime world.

DEPLOYED TO DO WHAT JESUS DID

The Bible describes a typical week in Jesus' life like this:

Jesus went through all the towns and villages, teaching in their synagogues, proclaiming the good news of the kingdom and healing every disease and sickness. When he saw the crowds, he had compassion on them, because they were harassed and helpless, like sheep without a shepherd." (Matthew 9:35-36)

In this passage, we see what Jesus did and His heart behind it. The Gospels often describe Jesus as someone who had compassion, and this passage says His heart was moved because He realized how harassed and helpless people were. Don't you just love this about Jesus? When Jesus deploys us, He gives us a heart for the hurting people in our world, and we can't help but have compassion on them.

But let me just say that having a heart for people is only the launchpad for the things we get to do as people who are sent. This passage tells us that Jesus went around "proclaiming the good news of the kingdom and healing every disease and sickness." The same thing happened when Jesus "called the twelve together…and sent them forth to preach the kingdom of God and heal the sick" (Luke 9:2). Then He sent out the 72, telling them to "heal the sick who are there and tell them, 'The kingdom of God has come near to you'" (Luke 10:9). When Peter preached the good news at Pentecost, 3000 people got saved, and Scripture says the people were "filled with awe at the many wonders and signs performed by the apostles" (Acts 2:43).

And so it has been for over two thousand years. We get to share the good news of salvation and pray for miracles so people will know that the kingdom of God has come. Supernatural experiences like healing or deliverance demonstrate that there is no God like ours! All over the world, people all are coming to faith in Jesus Christ because they've seen signs and wonders and heard the truth about Jesus' death for their sins. It is incredible that we get to be a part of this! Jesus has deployed us to do what He did: to preach the good news of salvation to a lost world and to help heal their physical, emotional and spiritual brokenness by bringing His kingdom.

DEPLOYED TO GET THE GOSPEL TO THE ENDS OF THE EARTH

Jesus gave a final deployment message to the disciples as He was about to return to heaven, saying: "But you will receive power when the Holy Spirit comes on you; and you will be my witnesses in Jerusalem, and in all Judea and Samaria, and to the ends of the earth" (Acts 1:8). This wasn't a new idea to the disciples. As we saw in our chapter on making disciples, Jesus had already told them to "Go and make disciples of all nations…." Earlier He'd said they were going to experience some really tough things, but then he promised them this: "And this gospel of the kingdom will be preached in the whole world as a testimony to all nations, and then the end will come" (Matthew 24:14).

Jesus was making a huge claim, that history as we know it will come to an end once every nation has heard the gospel. You and I are not just off on our own little deployment—we get to be a part of God's plan to reach all the nations of the world! This is what heaven is all about, as Jesus showed the Apostle John in a vision:

After this I looked, and there before me was a great multitude that no one could count, from every nation, tribe, people and language, standing before the throne and before the Lamb. They were wearing white robes and were holding palm branches in their hands. And they cried out in a loud voice: "Salvation belongs to our God, who sits on the throne, and to the Lamb." (Revelation 7:9-10)

Here's the crazy thing. For the first time in history, we are at the point where every tribe, people, and tongue can actually be reached with the good news of Jesus. I recently sat in on a conference with an organization called *Finishing the Task*, which is a group of missions organizations and churches that have come together, and through the use of satellite imaging and artificial intelligence have identified every single ethno-linguistic people group on earth. During that conference, the last people group on their list was adopted by some believers who are committed to getting the gospel to them.

Are you seeing this? You could be the generation that ushers in the return of Jesus. You may not go to the ends of the earth, but you get to help make it happen. How? You can pray, you can give, you can go on a short-term missions' trip, you can support missionaries, and some of you will actually pack your bags and go for the long haul. The point is, Jesus has deployed us all to work together to reach every tribe and tongue with the Gospel, and once that happens, He is coming back.

I don't know about you, but I want Jesus to come back. I look at this dying world and I see the pain and the suffering. I see more human slavery than in the time of the Transatlantic Slave Trade. I see more suicide than any time in history. I see a raging epidemic of bondage to pornography. I see crazy greed and materialism. I see sexual morality completely disintegrating, families torn to shreds and total confusion about what is truth and what values even matter anymore. I also see a people distracted like never before. It is crazy what has happened in just a few decades with technology. Not only are our brains being rewired in harmful ways, but our bodies are physically changing because of our addictions to our phones and digital devices.

So yes, I long for Jesus to come back, but in the meantime, you and I are deployed to bring His kingdom here and now, until He returns. This will take something that is almost unheard of in this day and time — people who will deny themselves and take up their crosses like Jesus did, to become like Him in His death. There's never been a harder time to die to your own will and desires than in this generation. You can sit in your room and let the world come to you — you can be entertained or have food delivered or play video games or text endlessly or immerse yourself in social media for hours every day without ever looking up or out. You can absolutely waste your life and not even know it.

DEPLOYED TO ACTIVE DUTY IN A WARTIME WORLD

This brings me to the final point about deployment, which is that you are called to active duty in a war that began before this world was created and will not end until Jesus returns. The summer Stef and I got married, we took off to Southeast Asia to lead missions teams in Indonesia and Sri Lanka. We had a one-week break in between, so we headed to the tropical island chain of the Maldives for vacation. It had been a crazy busy semester of work, and then everyone knows pulling off a wedding is no small feat, so I was very excited to have some time to relax on a beautiful beach. But things didn't go quite how we expected. At the airport upon entry there was a sign forbidding Bibles or other religious materials. I hid my Bible and kept going.

We got to the resort that evening and were taken to our Bungalow and things went downhill from there. I can only describe that evening as the worst of my life. All I can say is that I was demonically attacked while trying to sleep that night. I felt a lot of oppression on my body and then I began to see all kinds of demonic images crawling on the ceiling. I had to wake up my sweet bride, who desperately tried to stay up with me as I was traumatized by the experience and couldn't sleep.

As I prayed the next morning and asked God what was going on, I heard a still, small voice, and I will never forget what He said: "Son you can't come into a war zone— a place of stronghold for the enemy, a place where he has had a strong grasp, and just relax and take a vacation. You have to fight." So, Stef and I checked out of the resort and took a boat to the capital city to do our own version of a mission trip. We would spend the mornings in prayer and intercession over this country that had no known believers, no church and no missionaries that we knew of. Then in the afternoon we went out asking God to direct our steps.

Our first afternoon we made friends with a young waiter who'd been a professional athlete in that county. We ended up spending much of the rest of the week with him and his friends, even going into his village. At one point the young man explained that he dropped out of soccer because of an ankle injury that still affected him. I asked if I could pray for him, and right there in front of his friends laid my hands on his ankle and prayed. Immediately after I finished, he looked at me in wide eyed wonder and said: "You're a magician!" as he moved around excitedly declaring he'd been completely healed. I told him I wasn't a magician, but this was the power of Jesus, the power of the One I'd been telling him about. That day he gave his life to Jesus.

It was not an easy week, but it was a victorious one. That week the war for souls became real to me. In John's vision we read about above, every tribe and tongue is worshipping around the throne, but he also had a vision of another scene that happened long ago:

Then war broke out in heaven. Michael and his angels fought against the dragon, and the dragon and his angels fought back. But he was not strong enough, and they lost their place in heaven. The great dragon was hurled down — that ancient serpent called the devil, or Satan, who leads the whole world astray. He was hurled to the earth, and his angels with him. (Revelation 12:7-9)

There was a war in heaven. We know this happened. Satan wanted to be worshipped like God, and thus he was hurled down. But where to? This is where people are confused. They do not understand that Satan was hurled to earth. According to Scripture, Satan is the prince of the power the air and the god of this world (Ephesians 2:2, 2 Corinthians 4:4). People have too low of a view of Satan — they think he isn't real or is hanging out in hell. But let me just tell you — the reason there is so much destruction, hate, rape, genocide, terrorism, murder and on and on is because Satan is at war with the people of God and will do everything he can to keep us from bringing Jesus' kingdom to the darkness in this world.

We are at war, and you have been deployed to active duty! Although Jesus said, "I will build my church and the gates of hell will not prevail against it," it feels like the hordes of hell are destroying the earth. Why? Because we don't live like the devil is on our doorstep, waging war against us. We've been lulled to sleep by our own wants and desires, our own hunger for comfort and insatiable appetites. We've come to believe that following Jesus is just about making our life a little more pleasant.

One time on a long flight, I watched the movie *Captain America*, and it absolutely captivated my heart. The premise is that there is this young, weak guy with a huge heart who can't get into the military but gets chosen to receive a serum that will amplify what is in his heart. Ultimately, he becomes Captain America — strong, intelligent and courageous. When his best friend and others are held captive behind enemy lines and no one else is willing to take the risk, out of loyalty and love Captain America goes fearlessly on a mission to rescue them from destruction.

Everyone loves Captain America. But do you realize that God has made this your story and mine? We feel weak and inadequate, but Jesus wants to clothe us with supernatural power from the Holy Spirit, so we can be a part of his end times rescue mission! Scripture says: "This is good, and pleases God our Savior, who wants all people to be saved and to come to a knowledge of the truth" (1 Timothy 2:3-4). Right now, there are people who need rescuing all over the world, who need to know the truth about God's love for them. God wants to save them from eternal destruction, and He's calling you to active duty to go behind enemy lines and bring them home. Then and only then will you be who you are called to be.

Has the war become real for you? Do you wake each day, knowing that there is a battle ahead, that there is an enemy who rules this world and will fight to keep you from rescuing others? I want you to know that Jesus is stronger, that you are an overcomer because "the one who is in you is greater than the one who is in the world?" (1 John 4:4).

But still, we have to fight! Please don't live your life in a battle zone trying to relax. Go across your office, across your street, across your classroom, and even across your living room to fight for the souls of men and women and children that Jesus longs to save! You are not alone — the Holy Spirit fills you with power, and your fellow soldiers are all around you, ready to join arms to win the victory! War is upon us. You are deployed!

PARTING THOUGHTS

My dad has never been much of a communicator. In fact, I can't think of one time in my life where I heard him address an audience. He was a deacon in the church I grew up in, and the tradition was that the deacons would rotate each service, walking up that long center aisle to stand at the microphone in front of the large wooden pulpit and say the offering prayer. That was what all the deacons did. Except my dad. He was highly respected, just not one to speak publicly. So, you can imagine my great surprise when he stood up at my wedding reception with a microphone in his hand to speak.

People say no one remembers their wedding day. They are wrong! I remember that moment and just become emotional all over again, as if it just happened. Dad pulled out a letter from his coat pocket and began to read. He recounted many of the adventures we had together hunting and fishing. We were avid outdoorsmen and I loved those times. He shared how I had been his only son, so it had always been just him and me going far and wide to find "the big one," which meant the trophy buck. But then Dad transitioned and, looking right at me, said: "All those years of hunting for the *big* one, of going after the trophy, and I realized I had it with me right there all along. Robert, you are that trophy."

Wow. I just melted. What more does a son want to hear from his father? You see I knew hunting had been one of my dad's greatest loves since childhood. He chose his college largely because there was good hunting nearby, and he had an entire closet in our house devoted to all things hunting. We had hunting magazines, hunting videos, and went on a ton of hunting trips. Of course I knew that I meant more than hunting did to my dad, but at that moment, in front of all our friends and family, for him to look at me and say that I was the greatest prize, his trophy, the big one that he had pursued all his life, I felt like my heart would explode. To know that I was more exciting to him, that time with me was more fulfilling, and that having me in his life was more rewarding than the thing he was so devoted to made me feel loved and cherished beyond comprehension.

Why do I tell this story? I want you to know that this is just a small picture of how God feels about you and me. Your heavenly Father loves you far more than any earthly father can. I believe if your spiritual eyes were opened, you'd see God standing there at the biggest gathering of your life, in front of all your friends and family, looking you in the eyes and saying: "My son, my daughter, you are my prize. You are the one I love and cherish."

Friend, I don't want you to miss the whole point of this little book. The five Ds are not a checklist for you to cross off so you can feel good about yourself or measure up to someone's religious standard. They are a road map that will lead you on a lifelong journey right into the presence and arms of God. My desire as your move through these five — Decision, Dunked, Discipled, Delivered, Deployed — is that you will fall in love with the beauty and wonder of Jesus, who walks with you step by step, and discover that you are cherished by your Heavenly Father as you draw closer to Him than you ever imagined possible.

SMALL GROUP/MENTOR DISCUSSION QUESTIONS

CHAPTER ONE: DECISION

1. Share with each other whether you have made a personal decision to follow Jesus as Lord and Savior. If you have, when did this happen, and how? What has been the most meaningful part of this for you? If you haven't, what do you think might be holding you back?

2. Of the four things Jesus gives us at salvation, which one most encourages you and why? (spirituality, identity, purity, destiny)

3. Which of the four things do you struggle with or have questions about? Why?

4. Read Romans 10:9-10 below from *The Passion Translation* of the Bible:

    For if you publicly declare with your mouth that Jesus is Lord and believe in your heart that God raised him from the dead, you will experience salvation. The heart that believes in him receives the gift of the righteousness of God — and then the mouth gives thanks to salvation.

What stands out most to you in this? What does it tell us about how we receive salvation? What thoughts and feelings does this passage stir in you?

CHAPTER TWO: INTRODUCING THE 5 Ds

1. Where are you on the 5 "Ds" Growth path? Which step seems the most challenging for you and why?

2. What do you think your next step needs to be?

3. Has your journey so far with Jesus been more like going to a movie theater or a gym? In what ways?

4. Read the following words of Paul from the Message Bible:
   God knew what he was doing from the very beginning. He decided from the outset to shape the lives of those who love him along the same lines as the life of his Son. The Son stands first in the line of humanity he restored. We see the original and intended shape of our lives there in him. Romans 8:28
   How does Paul describe what God wants to do in us? What do you think this means?

5. What does the passage below tell you about following Jesus?
   Here's how we can be sure that we know God in the right way: Keep his commandments. If someone claims, "I know him well!" but doesn't keep his commandments, he's obviously a liar. His life doesn't match his words. But the one who keeps God's word is the person in whom we see God's mature love. This is the only way to be sure we're in God. Anyone who claims to be intimate with God ought to live the same kind of life Jesus lived. 1 John 2:2-6

6. What steps are you taking right now to follow Jesus and live the same kind of life Jesus lived?

CHAPTER THREE: THE SECOND "D" – DUNKED

1. What are some reasons you have heard people give for not being baptized in water? Do these reasons spring from religion or relationship?

2. Why do you think churches (and people) have required people to take certain steps before being baptized? Why do you think the Bible shows it can (and should) happen immediately?

3. What experiences have you had regarding the baptism with the Holy Spirit? Did you pray the prayer at the end of the chapter? If so, share about this.

4. What do you feel you have gained through baptism in the Holy Spirit? (Power, gifts etc.) How did it change you?

5. How would you encourage someone who felt they didn't need to be baptized with the Holy Spirit?

6. Read the following passage about the baptism with fire from *The Message Bible:*
   But who will be able to stand up to that coming? Who can survive his appearance? He'll be like white-hot fire from the smelter's furnace. He'll be like the strongest lye soap at the laundry. He'll take his place as a refiner of silver, as a cleanser of dirty clothes. He'll scrub the Levite priests clean, refine them like gold and silver, until they're fit for God, fit to present offerings of righteousness. Then, and only then, will Judah and Jerusalem be fit and pleasing to God, as they used to be in the years long ago. Malachi 3:2-4
   The Bible teaches that when we invite Jesus to be our Lord and Savior, we become priests with full access to Him. What does this passage tell us will happen to God's priests when He comes to refine us by fire? What will be the result?

7. Have you ever experienced this? If so, what was it like? What was the result? If not, what might be some reasons to ask for it?

CHAPTER FOUR: THIRD "D" – DELIVERED

1. Discuss what ideas come to mind when you think of the word *deliverance*. Can you share a story of a time when Jesus delivered you?

2. Why do you think followers of Jesus often don't experience deliverance? What do you think keeps people from living in freedom?

3. David had to let go of three things to experience deliverance: self-reliance, self-justification and control. Which do you struggle with most? Why?

4. Read the following passage (James 4:6-10) from *The Passion Translation:*

    But he continues to pour out more and more grace upon us. For it says, "God resists you when you are proud but continually pours out grace when you are humble." So then, surrender to God. Stand up to the devil and resist him and he will turn and run away from you. Move your heart closer and closer to God, and he will come even closer to you. But make sure you cleanse your life, you sinners, and keep your heart pure and stop doubting. Feel the pain of your sin, be sorrowful and weep! Let your joking around be turned into mourning and your joy into deep humiliation. Be willing to be made low before the Lord and he will exalt you!

    List the instructions that James gives related to deliverance. What promises does he give us?

5. Share with each other any areas where you feel like you might need deliverance. Based on what you have learned in the chapter, take time to personally repent and release, and then pray for each other. Use the prayer at the end of the chapter for anyone who hasn't gone through it yet, or feels they need more deliverance.

CHAPTER FIVE: FOURTH "D" – DISCIPLED

1. Share together any experiences you have had in being discipled or making disciples. What is one encouraging story?

2. Why do you think people in many churches never get discipled or go make disciples?

3. Read the following verses and list any elements of a discipling relationship that you see:

   The student is not above the teacher, but everyone who is fully trained will be like their teacher. Luke 6:40

   What you heard from me, keep as the pattern of sound teaching, with faith and love in Christ Jesus. Guard the good deposit that was entrusted to you — guard it with the help of the Holy Spirit who lives in us. 2 Timothy 1:13-14

   And the things you have heard me say in the presence of many witnesses entrust to reliable people who will also be qualified to teach others. 2 Timothy 2:2

   I long to see you so that I may impart to you some spiritual gift to make you strong — that is, that you and I may be mutually encouraged by each other's faith. Romans 1:11-12

4. How do you respond to the teaching that when a follower of Christ does not make disciples, he or she is in disobedience? What would keep you from entering into a discipleship relationship, if anything?

5. Share together your next steps related to making disciples (join a small group, start a small group, ask someone to disciple you, ask someone to let you disciple them, etc.).

CHAPTER SIX: FIFTH "D" – DEPLOYED

1. Review the definitions above of "occupation" and "vocation." Share together how you see your occupation and how you see your vocation. How do these fit together as someone who has been deployed by Jesus?

2. What does it mean that we are deployed to do what Jesus did? In what ways do you try to practice this? What are your struggles with this?

3. What part do you see yourself playing in being deployed to get the Gospel to the ends of the earth? What next steps could you take to be sure you are involved?

4. Do you think you live your life as one in a war zone, with an active duty mentality? Why or why not?

5. Jesus announced the following as His mission on earth. Read it together and then share what stands out to you, given that Jesus says He is sending you as His Father sent Him:

   The Spirit of the Lord is on me, because he has anointed me to proclaim good news to the poor. He has sent me to proclaim freedom for the prisoners and recovery of sight for the blind, to set the oppressed free, to proclaim the year of the Lord's favor. Luke 4:18-19

6. Walk through a normal weekday in your life and share what you think would be different if you really took seriously the reality that Jesus has deployed you. Pray for each other as each one shares.